MISSISSIPPI ARCHAEOLOGY

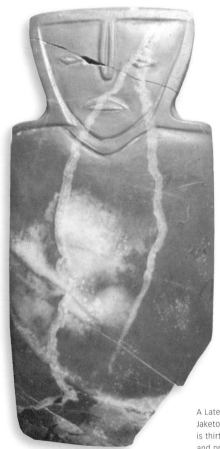

A Late Archaic–period stone tablet from the Jaketown site, Humphreys County. This artifact is thirteen centimeters (about five inches) long and probably dates to between about 1000 and 1500 B.C. Photo courtesy of the Mississippi Department of Archives and History.

MISSISSIPPI ARCHAEOLOGY

EVAN PEACOCK

UNIVERSITY PRESS OF MISSISSIPPI / *JACKSON*

www.upress.state.ms.us

Designed by Todd Lape

The University Press of Mississippi is a member of the
Association of American University Presses.

Illustrations courtesy of Evan Peacock unless otherwise noted

First edition 2005
Library of Congress Cataloging-in-Publication Data

Peacock, Evan, 1961–
Mississippi archaeology Q & A / Evan Peacock.— 1st ed.
p. cm.
Includes index.
ISBN 1-57806-766-9 (alk. paper) — ISBN 1-57806-767-7 (pbk. : alk. paper)
1. Indians of North America—Mississippi—Antiquities—Miscellanea.
2. Mississippi—Antiquities—Miscellanea. 3. Archaeology—Mississippi—
Miscellanea. 4. Excavations (Archaeology)—Mississippi—Miscellanea.
5. Historic sites—Mississippi—Miscellanea. I. Title: Mississippi archaeology Q and A. II. Title: Mississippi archaeology questions and answers. III.
Title.
E78.M73P43 2005
976.2'01—dc22   2004024531

British Library Cataloging-in-Publication Data available

THIS BOOK IS DEDICATED TO JANET RAFFERTY,
WHO HAS TAUGHT ME AND SO MANY OTHERS
WHAT DEDICATION IS ALL ABOUT.

CONTENTS

ACKNOWLEDGMENTS

The number of people I would need to thank for helping me on this book in particular and in my career in general is so large that it would require a separate chapter to do them justice. My wife and colleague, Janet, and our children, David and Nicole Rafferty, top every list: they made my life better in every conceivable way. Nicole, Janet, and Charles Cooner provided very helpful editorial comments on a draft of this book. A number of archaeologists, professional and avocational, provided assistance: David Abbott, Jeffrey Alvey, Keith Baca, Oded Borowski, Sam Brookes, Kevin Bruce, Suzanne Bufkin, Ken Carleton, Phil Carr, John Connaway, Jack Elliott, Carey Geiger, Bruce Gray, Ed Jackson, Sam McGahey, Jim Turner, John Underwood, Lizbeth Velasquez, and Amy Young. I owe a special debt of gratitude to Cliff Jenkins for his consummate professionalism and never-ending willingness to help. I would like to thank Ken P'Pool and Chrissy Wilson of the Mississippi Department of Archives and History and Russ Houston, Mississippi State University, for their assistance with figures. Additional assistance with figures was provided by the Minerals Management Service, U.S. Department of the Interior—special thanks to Jack Irion—and Claudia Jew of the Mariners' Museum in Newport News, Virginia. Homes Hogue has been a most excellent collaborator, mentor, and friend, and I am privileged to work with her and Ron Loewe, our cultural anthropologist at Mississippi State University. I would like to thank the members of the Sorrels family for their hospitality at the Lyon's Bluff site, and Dick Marshall and Jay Johnson and his students, especially Matthew Reynolds and Brian Haley, for their assistance there. Pat Galloway deserves recognition for her long years of service to the Mississippi Archaeological Association, as do so many members of that fine organization. Terry Winschel and Patty Montague of the Vicksburg National Military Park provided information relating to looting at that important site. I would like to thank John Baswell and all the gang at the Tombigbee National Forest for the many happy and productive years that I worked there. The Cobb Institute of Archaeology at Mississippi State has been a second home in one way or another since 1984. I would like to thank Dr. Joe Seger, the director of the Cobb, for supporting my research and for providing opportunities for our students. I would like to thank the Archaeological Conservancy, and Alan Gruber and Jessica Crawford in particular, for the exemplary service they have done in preserving important sites in our state and elsewhere. Archaeology students are a breed apart, and I have been fortunate to know and work with several generations of them at MSU. I would like to thank Jeffrey Alvey, Valerie Davis, and Tom James for serving as field assistants at Lyon's Bluff.

Finally, I would like to recognize Dennis, Bennie, Hardy, Glenn, Robert, and Andy, who got to share with me the unforgettable experience of growing up in the backwoods of Choctaw County, where dirt-clod wars and escaped hogs were among the more common recreational events for a happy band of brothers.

MISSISSIPPI ARCHAEOLOGY

ARCHAEOLOGY—
THE STUDY OF "STUFF"

I was about ten years old when I found my first prehistoric artifact. I found it in Choctaw County, Mississippi, about four miles west of the town of French Camp. In what turned out to be a bit of ironic good fortune, my brother Bennie, home on leave from the navy, happened to be filming out in the backyard of our home at the time. The 8-mm film shows a towheaded, barefoot, shirtless boy, blonde as corn silk, walking in a small garden about eighty yards away. The boy stops, stoops, straightens . . . and then comes running toward the house at full speed, a treasure clutched in one pumping fist. He reaches the camera, holds his hand out, and opens it to reveal . . .

Nothing. Precisely at that moment, the film ran out.

Although it was not captured on film, the moment was certainly captured in my memory for all time. The artifact was my first arrowhead—and from that point on I was "runt" for anything besides archaeology, as one might say in Choctaw County. I have found many points and other artifacts since, at many places in Mississippi and other states and countries, but none quite matched that first find on a north Mississippi truck farm so many years ago. Some twelve years later, having begun my formal education in archaeology, I recorded that first find with the

Mississippi Department of Archives and History. One perk of reporting a site is that you get to name it. It was with what I hope is forgivable hubris that the first archaeological find I ever made is now officially registered as "Peacock 1."

Mississippi is a fascinating place to work; it has an extraordinarily rich archaeological record, with many important sites in every

The author holding a stone arrowhead made of Kosciusko quartzite. Many people mistakenly refer to these small artifacts as "bird points."

county. I am very fortunate to have had the opportunity to work in the state, and I have tried to take advantage of that opportunity. For the last twenty years, I have devoted almost every day of my life to archaeology, as a student, as a practitioner, and as a teacher. Part of my job has been to give talks to people young and old all over the state. I have been gratified at the intense interest that people have shown in the topic; no small number have fond memories of their own finds out in the fields of their home counties. It is because of their interest and encouragement that I decided to write this book. I hope that it will educate as well as entertain. For there most certainly is a need for education. Do you have a cigar box, or bucket, or shoebox, or some other handy container full of arrowheads sitting in a closet? Do you have a piece of wood with arrowheads glued to it, perhaps arranged in a pleasing pattern? Did you know that picking those artifacts up in one way means that you have made a valuable contribution to understanding the archaeology of Mississippi, but picking them up in another way means that you have pretty much thrown away whatever could be learned from them? Have you ever

Clarksdale

Oxford

Ingomar
Mounds

Pharr
Mounds

Tupelo

Denton

Owl Creek
Mounds

Winterville
Mounds

Grenada

Bynum
Mounds

Lyon's Bluff

Greenville

Starkville

Columbus

Jaketown

Little
Spanish
Fort

Nanih
Waiya

Vicksburg

Meridian

Vicksburg
Military
Park

Jackson

Blaine Mound
(destroyed)

Natchez

Grand Village
of the Natchez,
Saragossa Plantation

Hattiesburg

The locations of some of the archaeological sites
mentioned in this book.

The Josephine

wanted to know more? If so, then there is something in this book for you.

Another reason for writing this book is that very little nontechnical information is currently available for interested people. Take, for example, that first arrowhead mentioned above. Looking at it now, I immediately recognize it as a Late Woodland–period arrow point, fashioned between about A.D. 700 and 1000 out of Kosciusko quartzite, a particularly intractable, steel-gray rock that, despite its toughness, was in common use at the time. The distribution of artifacts made from this particular raw material is limited to near the Kosciusko formation, a geological bed that runs in a narrow belt down the central part of the state. The fact that artifacts of "KQ" aren't found far from the source suggests that it was never an important material for prehistoric trade. Several blocky "steps" occur near the middle of the point; these breaks reflect the difficulty of working such a tough rock. They also suggest that the maker wasn't worried about making a product that was too aesthetically pleasing, just something that worked.

Now, if I had written at the outset that I had a Late Woodland–period, excurvate-bladed triangular *projectile point* of Kosciusko quartzite displaying multiple step fractures near the median ridge, most people wouldn't know what on earth I was talking about. If, on the other hand, I had mentioned finding a "bird point," many readers would immediately have formed a picture in their minds (a somewhat inaccurate picture, as it happens—see chapter 8). So I would like for this book to educate, and toward that end I have italicized many words that carry a technical meaning. These are listed along with their definitions in a glossary at the end of the book, and some are explained in sidebars. But the book itself is written in a nontechnical fashion that will, I hope, be entertaining for the reader.

This book is not meant to be a comprehensive overview of all of the important sites and artifacts known in our state. That would certainly be a worthy project, and one that I hope will be undertaken in the future. In the meantime, I have tried to include enough specific examples to make this book at least something of an introduction to Mississippi's remarkable archaeology. I have tried to give at least some coverage to all the different parts of the state, but far more has been left out than I have been able to include. Regardless of where you live in Mississippi, rest assured that a rich archaeological record lies right outside your door. My hope is that this book will help you to understand and appreciate that record in new ways.

I've been among archaeologists for almost half my life, and I can still sit all night and listen to them talk. Archaeology is full of stories, and I have shared a few of my own in these pages that I hope you will find amusing. If this book succeeds on either front—education or entertainment—then I will in some small fashion have paid back the people of Mississippi for the opportunity to realize the dream of a young farm boy in Choctaw County so many years ago.

WHY DO WE DO ARCHAEOLOGY?

There are a million and one things we can spend money on in this world, some worthy, some not. *Archaeology* is, I firmly believe, one of the worthy ones. Compared to other countries and states, Mississippi spends very little on archaeology, but we do spend some. Where does that money come from? What happens to it? How is it spent? Does archaeology even matter so much that money should be spent doing it?

For starters, let me say that most archaeology is ultimately funded by taxpayers' dollars, one way or another. Because of this, most archaeologists (who are a very hard-working and conscientious group of people, by and large) spend a lot of time thinking about how to do their jobs in the most correct, defensible, and efficient manner possible. I had the opportunity to work as an archaeologist for the U.S. Forest Service in Mississippi for several years, and not a day went by that I didn't think hard about whether I was giving the taxpayers their money's worth. I currently work for a state university, and I keep that same responsibility in mind and make sure that my students understand it as well. The reason that tax money is spent on archaeology is because we have laws that say it must be done, something that will be further discussed in this book. If we have laws, then enough citizens considered archaeology sufficiently important to get those laws passed. My conclusion is that the best way for archaeologists to meet their obligations is to be the very best they can at what they do. We are not paid a lot, compared to many professions—one doesn't become an archaeologist to get rich—and what we do make we earn, through what can be very hard work indeed. But we don't starve either; a professional archaeologist certainly can make a comfortable living. And we are rewarded by the privilege of spending our lives doing something we care deeply about, in a business that rarely gets dull.

Why do archaeology? Well, let's begin with the long-term view. What does it mean to be human? That might seem like a silly question; you know what it means to be human—you are one. But if we look around the world, if we look across space and through time, we discover that we are only a very, very small part of humanity as a whole. There have been myriad cultures over the last three million years, beginning in Africa and gradually spreading out to cover the globe. Ours is an incredible and fascinating species. We have been phenomenally successful in occupying different habitats, in shaping our cultures to meet the multitudinous demands of different climates and locales. We have been hunters, gatherers, collectors, fishers, foragers, and farmers. We have been warriors, peacemakers, politicians, craftsmen, priests, mechanics, roofers, engineers, musicians, artists, and explorers. We have crossed vast deserts, climbed high mountains, and left our stamp upon woodlands, plains, tropical forests, and arctic wastes. We have crossed oceans, flown through the air, walked upon our moon, and sent our devices through the emptiness of space to view up close the desolate terrain of other planets. We are unique. Ours is, therefore, an existence well worth study.

So where do we begin? History provides us with much to go on. But history is the study of the written word, and although it gives us valuable insights into human beliefs and behavior over the last few thousand years, the vast majority of human existence took place before written languages existed. Almost all of what it means to be human lies beneath our feet, in the bits and pieces of things made and left behind over the ages. We can access that experience only through the practice of archaeology (the study of *artifacts*—things made or modified by human beings—and the relationships between them). The past is a great unknown, one that we are only just beginning to explore. This is, I believe, why so many people are interested in archaeology. You don't have to travel to another planet to discover the unknown. It is right here, all around us, everywhere we turn. And it is *us*.

Archaeology also has something to teach us about our role as the current inhabitants of the planet. Countless people, innumerable cultures, have come before us. They changed the world, with fire, axe, shovel, and plow. They shaped the face of the earth, felling forests, tilling the soil, burning off the landscape. The changes wrought by human actions have in some cases been beneficial; in many cases they have been catastrophic. We are the inheritors of what has resulted from those actions. It is our responsibility to recognize that future generations likewise will inherit from us. We have three million years of cultural interaction with nature from which we can seek inspiration, knowledge, and guidance. We would be foolish to ignore such a potent source of information.

Future generations also will inherit something of ourselves, if we choose to leave it to them. The forces of commercialism are changing our cultural landscape at an ever-increasing pace. Think about your own hometown. How has it changed in your lifetime? Are there parts of it that you would like to have preserved so that your children, and their children, might see what sort of world you inhabited? When I worked for the U.S. Forest Service I found hundreds of old house sites out in the woods. These were often marked by piles of sandstone and bricks where chimneys once stood, caved-in cisterns that once provided water for

WHAT IS ARCHAEOLOGY?

Archaeology is the scientific study of artifacts, items that past peoples shaped and left behind. Very little of what archaeologists deal with would be especially impressive to a layperson: gold, hidden tombs, and priceless art objects are much more the stuff of movies than the workaday reality of the discipline. Frankly, most of the things that we find and study are bits and pieces of refuse—in a word, garbage. Things like small pieces of pottery, fragments of animal bones, worn out or broken stone tools, and other waste materials are the stuff with which we work. Fortunately, you can tell a lot about people from their garbage if you learn to look at it in the right ways, which is what archaeological research is all about. And "archaeology" really has a better ring to it than "paleo-garbology."

Finding artifacts, either through surface collection or through excavation, is really the easy part. Figuring out what those artifacts were used for and explaining patterns in how they are distributed in space and time is where the job gets difficult. To do this, archaeologists draw upon an amazing range of scientific methods, from many disciplines. Like zoologists, we study bones. Like geologists, we study rocks. Like botanists, we study plants. Like pedologists, we study soils. We use X-rays, radiocarbon dating, chemical tests, computer models—anything that helps to move us ahead in our knowledge of the past.

Experimental archaeology is one way in which we come to have a better understanding of how artifacts were made, used, and discarded. The production of a single stone spear point, for example, leads to the creation of hundreds of small chips or flakes. Archaeologists thus are much more likely to find flakes than points at ancient sites. Studying the flakes produced in experiments helps us to learn more from the flakes left behind by prehistoric cultures.

Some archaeologists even study living groups of people, or, more precisely, they study how contemporary people make artifacts and how those artifacts get left behind. These *ethnoarchaeologists* have studied things like caribou kill-sites used by the Nunamiut Eskimo of the Arctic Circle and the remains of small, temporary camps used by nomadic !Kung bands in the Kalahari Desert in South Africa. While such studies have little direct bearing on the archaeology of prehistoric Mississippi, they do provide indirect evidence of the kinds of obstacles hunter-gatherers face in their daily lives, and can lead us to questions we might otherwise not think to ask.

Archaeologist Kevin Bruce holding a stone projectile point that he has made using traditional methods. Note the tools of stone and antler, and notice also the hundreds of small, white flakes that were created as a by-product.

The author standing by a sawdust pile in Choctaw County. This feature marks the spot where a small sawmill once stood.

A small, family cemetery in Chickasaw County. Hundreds of these abandoned cemeteries lie scattered throughout the state.

WHY DO WE DO ARCHAEOLOGY?

WHAT DID THE WORLD LOOK LIKE IN THE PAST?

One of the first things an archaeologist must pay attention to is the environment of his or her study area. Environment shapes culture in a variety of ways and at a variety of scales. One doesn't grow cotton in the Arctic Circle, for example; nor does one hunt fur seals in Mississippi. At a finer scale, much of our human technology evolved to protect us from the vagaries of an unpredictable natural world. Clothing, shelter, food storage, agricultural tools, and weapons all are designed to make our place in the world more productive and stable. And even now we are not immune from the effects of environmental changes: witness the recent deaths of thousands of people in France—a modern, industrialized country—that resulted from one uncommonly hot summer.

Clearly, then, archaeologists need to know what the environment looked like at whatever point in space and time they are studying. This can be very tricky, as, of course, the landscapes of today may look nothing like they did in the past. What did Mississippi look like five hundred years ago? Five thousand years ago? Ten thousand years ago?

Archaeologists tackle this problem by excavating, along with the artifacts they study, the remains of once-living organisms from the earth. Sometimes these remains are large and easily visible, as with the bones of game animals, for example. Sometimes they are quite small, as is the case with the bones of small mammals or charred plant seeds. Small land snails are particularly useful, as they represent a local area (snails don't travel far!) and as they were only rarely eaten by people, meaning that they weren't brought in as food from other environments, as some animals may have been. Evidence related to past environments is even obtainable at the microscopic scale, as is the case with the pollen produced by flowering plants. By combining these different types of information, archaeologists can get a good idea of what the landscape looked like in the past, and from there we can construct models of how humans interfaced with the environment.

A small land snail resting on a penny. This snail was recovered along with thousands of others from an archaeological site in Oktibbeha County. Once the species are identified, archaeologists can use the information to understand what the site looked like in the past.

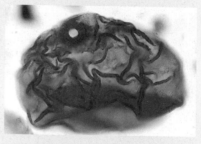

A grain of maize pollen magnified a thousand times. Archaeologists use the pollen from different kinds of plants to reconstruct past environments and to investigate how long-term human land use has altered the world. Photo courtesy of Gerald Kelso.

sharecropper families, isolated patches of ornamental flowers still maintaining their lonely and beautiful existence, and scattered artifacts such as plowshares, snuff bottles, and enameled chamber pots. Most of those sites are less than a hundred years old. How rapidly things change! Not so very long ago, many inhabitants of Mississippi had no electricity, no running water, no indoor toilets. They took their goods to town on wagons drawn by horses or mules. Oxen were used to haul timber to small "peckerwood" mills, while grain was ground at water-powered mills built astride energetic creeks. People lived, loved, worked, and died, and their remains lie in repose in hundreds of small family cemeteries hidden deep within the forests of the state. The visible remnants of that world are almost gone; it is a world our children will never know directly. It behooves us to preserve something of what is left, a memorial to the sweat and toil of those who came before us. It behooves us to save something of everything that makes Mississippi the special place that it is.

Archaeology does something else for us as well. It helps to bind us together into a common humanity. The artifacts themselves are interesting and important, but it was people, after all, who left them behind. As we learn more about the artifacts, we learn more about the people who made them. We are all inheritors of what it means to be human, and we, too, will leave our mark on the world. If part of our legacy is a greater understanding of what it all means, then our descendants will be justifiably proud of our achievements. And perhaps they won't have to work so hard to figure out what we were all about, generations after we, too, find repose in the deep forests and ancient soils of Mississippi.

HOW DO YOU KNOW
WHERE TO DIG?

The archaeological record of Mississippi is a vast, material phenomenon. It consists of enormous numbers of artifacts produced during thousands of years of human occupation, from the end of the last Ice Age right up until today. These artifacts lie strewn about the landscape, sometimes visible, sometimes hidden by soil and vegetation. Archaeologists refer to any place where artifacts are found as a *site*. How do we find sites, and, having found them, how do we determine which ones are worthy of further work and/or preservation? When we excavate a site, we very rarely dig all of it, for such an enterprise would be horrendously expensive. How, then, do we choose which part of any particular site to dig?

Sites are found in a number of ways. The most common is called *site survey*, in which archaeologists walk across the landscape systematically looking for artifacts on the surface, a technique called *open-field survey*, or digging small holes and screening the dirt. This latter technique is called *shovel-test survey* and is employed where vegetation or leaf litter hides the ground surface. Where do archaeologists go to do these surveys? That depends on what the reason is for doing surveys in the first

WHAT IS A SITE?

Archaeologists call any place where artifacts are found a site. Sites can be extremely small. For example, it is fairly common to find single, isolated spear points out in plowed fields. Sites also can be extremely large, as is the case with many prehistoric villages and "extinct" historic towns, for example. While "site" is a useful concept from a management standpoint—for example, the Mississippi Department of Transportation can design a highway so as to avoid an important site—the term really is not that useful for archaeologists. Why not? Because different groups of people might occupy the same ground at vastly different times, in which case their artifacts would be partly or completely overlapping. In other words, their artifacts would be found at the same site but would be otherwise unrelated. In response to this problem, archaeologist Robert Dunnell developed the concept of *occupation*, which refers to the artifacts that were deposited by a group of people over a period of continuous site use. With careful work, archaeologists can sometimes distinguish these separate occupations, even if they lie very close to one another on the same site.

WHAT IS A FEATURE?

Archaeologists may encounter a variety of features when they excavate. A feature is some kind of artifact that is too big, or has too many parts, or is too fragile to carry. A fire hearth is a good example of a feature; so is a mound. Concentrations of artifacts, such as piles of trash, also are features. Even a building can be considered a feature. In some countries, features are relatively easy to find archaeologically: ruins of ancient stone buildings, for example. In Mississippi, features can be very subtle, often being just dark stains in the soil. It takes a trained eye and many years of experience to become proficient at spotting and properly excavating features, as well as interpreting what they mean.

A pit feature at a Native American site in Oktibbeha County. The feature, when first found, was a dark, circular stain in the soil. One half has been removed, and artifacts, including deer and turtle bones and pieces of pottery, are exposed in the bottom of the pit. Photo courtesy of Janet Rafferty.

MISSISSIPPI FOCUS THE INGOMAR MOUNDS SURVEY PROJECT

The first survey I participated in happened in 1984, when I was an undergraduate student at Mississippi State University. The archaeologist in charge, Dr. Janet Rafferty, was trying to understand a very important and very interesting group of prehistoric mounds near the town of Ingomar, in Union County. At least six and perhaps as many as twelve mounds were built there about two thousand years ago. Most were conical burial mounds (more about those in chapter 7), but one—the magnificent Mound 14—is one of the largest Indian mounds in the Southeast, a thirty-foot-tall, flat-topped monument with a ramp leading off the northeast side. Obviously, a lot of work went into clearing the land and building so many mounds over an area of some eighty acres. What made that particular spot so important? How many people were involved in constructing the mounds? What was the purpose of Mound 14?

To try to answer those questions, Dr. Rafferty needed to know how many archaeological sites approximately the same age as the Ingomar Mounds were in the area. Accordingly, she took a map of Union and Pontotoc counties and, using Ingomar as a center point, drew a ten-kilometer-radius circle. Within that circle she randomly chose several quarter sections (160-acre, square parcels of land) to be surveyed. This type of approach is known as *random sampling*. If done correctly, the method gives a good representation of the number and types of sites in the chosen area. Once the survey plots were chosen, she assembled her students (me being one of them), and we set off into the soybean and cotton fields, maps and collection bags in hand. The farmers and other landowners were exceptionally gracious, in almost every case allowing us to look on their land to see what we could find. And what we found, among other things, were many small habitation sites about the same age as the mounds but scattered around the countryside. This finding suggested that the mound site itself was a central place, a focal point for an entire prehistoric *settlement pattern*. The artifacts from those open-field surveys formed the basis for one of the first systematic studies of the prehistoric remains of interior north Mississippi, a testament to the hospitality and curiosity of the people whose lands we walked.

Mound 14 at the Ingomar Mounds site. This flat-topped, Middle Woodland–period mound is one of the largest Indian mounds in the Southeast. The vehicles parked at the base of the mound provide an idea of the scale of this impressive earthwork. Photo courtesy of Janet Rafferty.

place. They can be done purely for research purposes, to try to learn something about what people were doing at a particular time and place in the past. Archaeologists also survey land that is going to be disturbed. In fact, this is why most surveys are done, and it is one way that archaeologists make their living. There are several laws in this country that say it's not OK to go out on public lands—or to use public money—to disturb the ground without looking first to see what's there. It's the same rationale that compels us to make sure that we don't wipe out any endangered species when we build a new reservoir. I will discuss these laws more fully in chapter 9. But for now, it's important to realize that, when you drive down that stretch of new highway that

The author digging a shovel test in Marshall County. In an effort to find unknown archaeological sites, hundreds of such tests might be dug in a project area. The dirt from each test is screened for artifacts.

finally opened, archaeologists traveled the route first—probably digging holes all the way!

When archaeologists find sites, they take great pains to record a lot of information about what they see and the artifacts that they collect. Most sites will be visited by an archaeologist only once (there are many more sites than there are archaeologists!), so we take the opportunity to learn

Mississippi State University students collecting artifacts from a prehistoric site in Lee County. Photo courtesy of Janet Rafferty.

as much as possible while we are there. The kinds of things that are typically recorded include site location, size, number of artifacts, distance to permanent water, soil conditions, how well preserved the site seems to be, the kinds of artifacts recovered, whether any visible *features* (nonportable artifacts such as mounds, chimney piles, standing structures, graves, cisterns, and so on) are present, the attitude of the landowner concerning possible excavation, and more. Artifacts are collected in a *general surface collection* with an eye toward obtaining a *representative sample*. In other words, we don't pick up just the points or other "collectibles." We are not picking things up for personal collections; we are trying to obtain a scientific sample that can be used for study by archaeologists of all future generations (see chapter 11 to find out what happens to the artifacts we collect). A sample that included only points, such as many collectors have, would, in fact, be largely point*less* for sci-

Mississippi State University student Marian Roberts recording information about a newly discovered site in Union County. Photo courtesy of Janet Rafferty.

entific purposes (although there are some things that such a collection could tell us, *if* the points were collected in the right way, as discussed later in this book). Archaeologists try to pick up some of everything that's at a site, in approximately the same proportions that exist there. If there are a lot of *flakes* (small pieces produced in the making of flaked-stone tools, sometimes called "chips"), we pick up a lot of flakes. If a site has lots of pieces of smoothly ground sandstone (used to grind plant seeds and other foods), we pick up lots of those pieces. If it has pottery, we pick up pottery (mostly as broken pieces, or *sherds*). And, of course, we like to find points and other beautiful artifacts as much as anyone, especially as we know that those points will be available for study, teaching, museum displays, or other such uses in the future. Working hard, having fun, finding stuff, and making a lasting contribution all at the same time: it doesn't get much better than open-field survey.

Shovel-test survey is much more difficult, and produces much smaller samples of artifacts with which to work. In many situations, however, it is the only way to find sites without causing undue damage. As a Forest Service archaeologist I carried out surveys wherever the agency was planning activities that might disturb the ground, such as timber sales or the construction of roads, lakes, or trails. In the woods, one has little opportunity to spot artifacts on the ground, of course, so I would work my way through the project area digging shovel tests on *transects*, straight lines along which I dug holes at certain intervals (usually every thirty meters, or about thirty-five yards). Each shovel test was about as big around as a basketball. I would dig my holes to a depth of about a foot or until I hit clay subsoil, whichever came first. The clay subsoil is a natural soil layer that usually doesn't contain artifacts; archaeologists call such layers *sterile*. I would put the dirt from each test through a small screen with a mesh size of one-quarter inch that I carried with me. Only very small artifacts will fall through such a screen; most will be caught and revealed when the dirt is worked through.

A collection of artifacts recovered from a prehistoric site in Winston County by shovel testing. The pieces of pottery, fragments of stone tools, and other artifacts are used to determine the site's age and function.

When I found artifacts in my screen, I knew that I was on a site. I would then carefully dig several other tests on transects, to find the site's boundaries and to get a sample of artifacts that I could use to try to figure out the site's age and *function* (what activities took place there). At an old house site, for example, I might find a variety of artifacts such as nails, glass, pieces of plates and other dishes, buttons, marbles, knife blades—all kinds of bits and pieces of things that were lost or discarded when a share-cropper's cabin stood there. At a prehistoric village site I might find pottery, flakes, broken and whole spear and arrow points, stone drills, ground sandstone, and bits of animal bone. Some *special-purpose sites* had only one specific use, and the archaeology is accordingly different. At an old sawmill site, for example, I might find nails, old oilcans, saw blades, metal gears and other bits of machinery. At a prehistoric hunting camp I might find only a few flakes where a Native American hunter sharpened a stone spear point hundreds or thousands of years ago.

(An interesting question to ask an archaeologist is what is the weirdest thing he or she has ever found. My own personal best is a leg. I was doing a shovel-test survey for the Department of Housing and Urban Development in a patch of woods behind a housing complex in central Alabama when I found an entire prosthetic leg lying on the ground. Archaeologists sometimes let their imaginations roam free and speculate about the stories behind the artifacts that they find. On that occasion, I really didn't want to know.)

When surveys are done because there is going to be some impact to the land, archaeologists face a difficult decision: which sites, out of all the ones that they find, are: A) important enough to preserve (often an expensive and troublesome proposition) or excavate to learn what we can before the sites are destroyed (potentially a *very* expensive and troublesome proposition); or B) not important, so that it's OK for them to be destroyed. A great deal of training, knowledge, and experience goes into making that decision, which is one reason why one must go to school for several years to become a professional archaeologist (a process discussed at length in chapter 12, if you're interested in archaeology as a career). It is a weighty responsibility. If, as an archaeologist, you decide that a site is *significant,* then your client (a highway department, a federal or state agency, a farmer asking for a federal loan to do erosion control on his land—whoever hires you to do the job) must

What Is the National Register of Historic Places?

All countries today grapple with a variety of problems and issues, one of which is: how does a nation deal with its important historical properties? What makes a particular property significant? Who is in charge of keeping track of those properties and making sure they get the attention they deserve? The answers to these questions are spelled out in various laws and regulations that can generally be referred to as historic preservation laws.

Historic preservation laws began to be passed in the United States in 1906, in response to the commercial looting of many spectacular Pueblo Indian sites in the Southwest. Following World War II, the need for historic preservation legislation increased dramatically as our country embarked upon an unprecedented period of highway construction, urban renewal, and other activities that were destroying important historic and prehistoric sites. A group of influential citizens and congressmen toured Europe to see how countries there were dealing with their cultural properties. It became glaringly apparent that the United States was lagging far behind in such regards, and the need for a national historic preservation program was recognized. On October 15, 1966, President Lyndon B. Johnson signed the National Historic Preservation Act (NHPA) into law, and our country entered a proud new era of caring for the things that help make it special.

Section 106 of NHPA states that federal agencies (and state agencies, if they use federal money) must "take into account" the effects of their actions on any "district, site, building, structure, or object" that is eligible for listing on the National Register of Historic Places, a list maintained by the National Park Service. In practice, this means that archaeologists, architectural historians, and other specialists are hired to look at project areas prior to construction to make sure that historically important places aren't needlessly destroyed. A property can be considered eligible for the National Register for many reasons. It may be associated with an important event in our nation's history (like a Civil War battlefield, for example). It may be associated with the life of a person significant in our past. It may be a characteristic example of a certain style or type of property (for example, a dogtrot cabin) or represent the work of a master craftsman. Or it might be able to tell us something important about the prehistoric or historic past that we don't currently know. A property can be considered eligible at the national, state, or local level, any of which conveys some protection against federally funded demolition or other forms of disturbance. Many important sites have been saved as a result of this legislation, and citizens should be proud of the efforts our country has made to preserve these visible reminders of our common heritage.

either avoid the site or pay to have it tested. A *test excavation* usually means excavating just enough of a site to determine if it is indeed historically significant or not.

Sometimes after testing, sites are deemed to be ineligible. Ineligible for what? For listing on the *National Register of Historic Places.* This is a list, administered by the National Park Service, of properties considered to be important as part of our nation's heritage. Odds are you have a building in your town with a brass plaque affixed to the side proudly noting that the structure is listed on the National Register. But buildings aren't the only things that can be listed. Any site that can tell us something important about prehistory or history is eligible for listing: prehistoric mounds, village sites, quarries, historic houses, battlefields, roads, mills, and so on. There currently are about 170 archaeological sites in Mississippi listed on the National Register, and many, many more that are considered to be eligible for listing. When such an important site is discovered where a government-funded impact is going to take place—in a planned highway corridor, for instance—then something has to be done about it. Whenever possible, such sites should be avoided. Preservation is always better than excavation because archaeologists in the future will have much more sophisticated tools than we currently have at our disposal. When an important site can't be avoided, it must be *mitigated*—that is, the damage must be lessened as much as possible. In practice, mitigation of an archaeological site usually means full-scale excavation to save as much information as possible before it is destroyed. If, on the other hand, an archaeologist decides that a site is not significant, then he or she has, in essence, given permission for it to be destroyed. And *that* will certainly keep you up at night. As I tell my students, one can never get good enough at making such decisions; the learning process never ends.

So, the choice of which site to dig depends on whether you're doing research—and if so, which site might tell you what you want to know—

or whether you are mitigating an impact, in which case the site is chosen for you by being in the impact zone. But here's another question. Some archaeological sites in Mississippi cover tens of acres. Having chosen a particular site to work at, how do you know where on that site to dig?

There are several ways to approach this problem. You could use random sampling, as described above for survey but this time applied to an individual site. The site is gridded off with a surveying instrument and grid unit numbers are randomly chosen up to the point where a certain portion of the site—say, five percent—will be excavated, usually in square excavation units measuring one or two meters on a side. (A meter is a little over a yard—the metric system is standard in archaeology.) Randomly choosing excavation units is one way to try to get an unbiased (representative) sample of artifacts and features. But there may be visible clues that tell you where to dig. On a historic site, for

A prehistoric site in Oktibbeha County that has been gridded off for a controlled surface collection. Each flag marks the location of one point in a grid system and is numbered accordingly. Archaeologists use this method to keep track of where on the site the artifacts are from. Photo courtesy of Janet Rafferty.

example, a square depression or a line of half-hidden bricks might mark the location of a cellar. A prehistoric site might have an earthwork other than a mound—a raised embankment, for example, encircling the site like a defensive wall. Excavating might be a good way to figure out how old it is and whether it was built all at once or in a series of construction episodes. Another approach is to do a *controlled surface collection*. After the site is gridded off, all the artifacts are collected from the surface in each grid unit. These are washed and analyzed separately to maintain their *provenience* information (which grid unit are they from?), and maps are made that show the distribution of different kinds of artifacts across the site. The results can reveal a lot about the internal structure of a settlement. For example, a cluster of pottery and animal bone fragments might reveal where a prehistoric house once stood, while a concentration of flakes might show where stone tools were made. Besides being a remarkably accurate way to direct excavation efforts, a controlled surface collection also provides at least some information about the entire site, not just those parts where you choose to excavate.

Science is constantly evolving new methods for exploration, and the science of archaeology is no exception. In the last few decades, a number of devices have been developed that literally allow us to see into the ground. One such device is a *ground-penetrating radar* unit, which sends electromagnetic waves into the ground and reads the reflections as those waves bounce off buried objects. A collapsed well or buried cellar might show up well with this method. *Soil resisitivity* and *conductivity meters* measure how easily an electric current passes through the soil. A feature such as a garbage pit, well, or grave would hold more groundwater than surrounding soils, causing current to pass more quickly through it. Careful reading of the results shows where such features occur beneath the soil. Still another method is *magnetometry*. Different kinds of soils have different magnetic properties. Topsoil, for example,

Mississippi State University student Lacey Culpepper conducting a magnetometry survey at the Lyon's Bluff site in Oktibbeha County. Photo courtesy of Jeffrey Alvey.

is more magnetic than subsoil, so a deep pit dug by an Indian hundreds or thousands of years ago that subsequently became filled with topsoil will be more magnetic than the surrounding clay. Burned soil tends to be highly magnetic, so a prehistoric hearth or burned house has a very strong magnetic signature. The magnetometer can read those signatures and produce amazing images of what's under the ground.

We also do underwater archaeology in Mississippi, something that is greatly aided by technology. For example, in 1997 an archaeological firm from Tennessee was hired to investigate a shipwreck rumored to exist in Biloxi Bay, in Jackson County. Using a magnetometer and another device called a *sidescan sonar*, the archaeologists were able to locate and describe the remains of the hull. They then recovered a number of arti-

How often have archaeologists wished that they had the power to see beneath the ground's surface? To actually see what lay below, rather than digging blindly into the earth? Astonishingly, we can now do just that. New devices are opening up a world of exploration that would have seemed like science fiction not so long ago.

An excellent example of the power of this new technology is provided by the results of a magnetometer survey at Lyon's Bluff, a large archaeological site in Oktibbeha County. Members of a Native American farming culture occupied a village at Lyon's Bluff from about A.D. 1200 to 1650. Excavations there have provided thousands of artifacts that tell us much about the lifeways of those early inhabitants. But as the archaeologist investigating the site I faced a daunting problem. Lyon's Bluff is exceptionally well preserved and is in no current danger of destruction, thanks to the care and diligence of the landowners. How could I learn more about the site without doing further damage to it myself?

The answer was provided when Dr. Jay Johnson of the University of Mississippi came to the site in the summer of 2001. He and his students conducted a magnetometry survey, a method that creates an image of the different magnetic properties of soils. The image produced for Lyon's Bluff was astonishing: the shapes of prehistoric houses and a palisade, or defensive wall, could clearly be seen! In 2003, my students and I continued the magnetic survey with a new instrument obtained by Mississippi State University, and still more archaeological features were

revealed. We now know the precise locations where several Native American buildings once stood, and have discovered that at least two palisades were built at the site at different times. These remarkable images allowed us to fine-tune our archaeological investigations so that we were able to learn a great deal about a very important site while doing minimal damage to it.

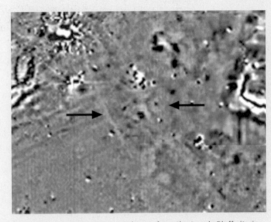

A portion of the magnetometer image from the Lyon's Bluff site in Oktibbeha County. The arrow on the left points to a long, white line: excavation showed this to be where a palisade, or defensive wall, once stood. The arrow on the right points to a square with a dark spot in the center. This is where a prehistoric house once stood. The dark spot inside the square is probably a central fire hearth. The house is about five meters (about sixteen feet) on a side.

The sidewheel steamship *Josephine* in 1867. Photo courtesy of the Mariners' Museum, Newport News, Virginia.

Not all archaeology lies in the ground. Beneath the waters of our rivers and lakes, and beneath the salty waves of the Gulf, there lie the wrecks of many vessels that went to the bottom as a result of weather, war, or sheer misfortune.

One such wreck is that of the sidewheel steamship *Josephine*. This beautiful ship was built in 1868 at the order of Charles Morgan, an ambitious New York shipping magnate who ran several routes in the Gulf of Mexico. On February 6, 1881, the ship was en route to New Orleans with a load of tobacco, cigars, and passengers from Cuba and Florida when disaster struck. A fierce storm caused a serious leak, which outpaced the bailing efforts of the passengers and crew. Early in the morning of February 8, the ship foundered and sank off the coast of Mississippi. Although no lives were lost, Morgan's loss at the time was estimated at seventy-five thousand dollars.

In 1997, archaeologists with the Minerals Management Service (MMS), a federal agency, took a sidescan sonar image of a known wreck that lay between Horn Island and Ship Island. The image clearly shows the exceptionally well-preserved wreck of a sidewheel steamship. The archaeologists further recorded their find using underwater photography. Based on comparisons of the wreck with published records, they were able to ascertain with certainty that they had indeed found the *Josephine*, one hundred and sixteen years after she went down. The wreck is now listed on the National Register of Historic Places, and remains an important time capsule from a bygone era.

A sidescan sonar image of the *Josephine* lying at the bottom of the Mississippi Sound. Image courtesy of the Minerals Management Service, U.S. Department of the Interior.

facts from the wreck, including bricks, wooden sheaves, and fragments of wooden barrels. Although it has not been identified with certainty, the vessel appears to be the remains of a colonial-period ship dating to the eighteenth century. The use of sidescan sonar and other "remote sensing" technology is becoming standard procedure in archaeology.

As wonderful as these devices are, they can tell the archaeologist only so much. To ascertain what's really down there in the ground—what it is, how deep it is, and how old it is—we still have to dig and spend a great deal of time analyzing our artifacts and trying to understand our data. Which is good. Because who would want to be an archaeologist if you couldn't get your hands dirty?

HOW DO YOU KNOW HOW OLD IT IS?

I get this one a *lot*. And a very good question it is. Often someone will bring in a stone spear point or arrowhead and ask me how old it is. Within a certain margin of error—a couple of hundred to several hundred years, depending on the type of object—I can usually tell at a glance how old a point, a piece of pottery, or some other *diagnostic* artifact is. A diagnostic is an artifact representative of a certain time period. How on earth do archaeologists know what kinds of artifacts go with what period? How do we know the dates of those periods? Sometimes we can date things—even very ancient things—to within less than a hundred years. It's a good trick, especially as it's not really a trick at all, but a very real part of the science of archaeology. So how do we do it?

Artifact forms tend to change in appearance over time. This is not something you need to be an archaeologist to notice: how different are the clothes that people wear today from what was in style a decade ago? Fifty years ago? A hundred? How have cars changed, or house styles, or any number of other artifact types? (For such things are artifacts just as surely as spear points or pieces of ancient pottery are.) In your lifetime, you will notice many such changes: imagine how much change occurs in a thousand lifetimes, or a thousand-thousand, and you begin to realize the magnitude of cultural change that archaeologists work with on a daily basis.

Detecting such changes is part of the business of archaeology. A more interesting—and much, much more difficult—task is explaining those changes. People were mobile hunters and gatherers for thousands and thousands of years. Why did our species leave Africa, the original home of all that we know as human? Why, ten thousand years ago, did we drastically change the way we relate to the world and become settled agriculturists, socially ranked city dwellers, an unwieldy conglomeration of haves and have-nots welded together with the rickety joints of bureaucracy and administration? Why do we have laws, music, theatre, football, war? Where have we been as a species, and where on earth—or even off of earth—are we going? At least some of those questions we may be able to answer, if archaeologists become good enough at what they do. A prerequisite for any such endeavor is to be able to control for time, to be able to take batches of stuff, assemblages of artifacts, and arrange them in chronological order so that change can be observed. As it happens, this is one thing that archaeologists are, in fact, very good at.

Something that I always try to impress upon my students is that there are many different ways of dating things. This is important, because if there

Drawings of projectile point types found in northeast Mississippi, showing how point styles change through time. Taken from the *Mississippi Projectile Point Guide*, by Sam McGahey, courtesy of the Mississippi Department of Archives and History (MDAH Archaeological Report No. 31).

were only one method—*radiocarbon dating*, for example—then archae-ologists could be criticized for accepting the results of that method at face value. When several different methods produce approximately the same results, however, it cannot be due to chance. This sort of cross-comparison is very valuable as we constantly work to improve our dating methods and our interpretations of the past that depend upon the results of those methods.

The most straightforward way of assigning an age to an artifact is by what we call *relative dating*. (This opens the door for various family reunion jokes, but as those tend to be overplayed in Mississippi, I will forbear.) In simple terms, relative dating is easy. Suppose you dig a hole in the ground. Right at the surface you find a stone arrowhead. Dig a foot deeper, and you find a different kind of stone point. Which one is older? The deeper one, of course, as it must have already been there when the second point was discarded. This is called the *Law of Superposition*: all other things being equal, younger stuff is higher and older stuff is lower in the earth. In practice, it often is not nearly so simple. In the hills of Benton and Marshall counties, I have found hundreds of small prehistoric sites, some on sandy soils that had artifacts at depths of as much as a meter. In that situation all of the artifacts were the same approximate age, but many had been moved downward in the loose, sandy soil by roots, worms, and other natural disturbances (archaeologists call this process *bioturbation*—"mixing by life"). Without recognizing this process, I might have thought that the deeper artifacts were much older. This is one reason why archaeologists are so careful when they excavate and record their finds: without such care, we might never figure out what was going on at any particular site.

A special kind of relative dating is called *cross-dating*. Let's say I excavate a site on the Tombigbee River and find a particular style of prehistoric pottery. In the same layer (or *stratum*) I also find charcoal from which I can get a radiocarbon date (we'll discuss this method further below). I send the charcoal to the lab, and I get back a date of A.D. 700. By association, I can say that pottery from the site dates to about that same time. If an archaeologist working in Alabama finds pottery that looks like mine, he can assume that it, too, dates to about A.D. 700 by comparison with my findings. Or he might get his own radiocarbon dates that show that the pottery style lasted until at least A.D. 850 in his area. Eventually enough dates are obtained so that we know the range within which particular artifact styles fall. So we know, for example, that pottery containing crushed mussel shell as *temper* (something added to the pot to help it shrink uniformly when it is dried and fired) began to be

An excavation unit at the Lyon's Bluff site in Oktibbeha County. The different layers visible in the photo are strata that contain artifacts. It can generally be assumed that artifacts from the deeper strata are older than the ones in higher strata.

made about a thousand years ago, at the beginning of what archaeologists have termed the Mississippi period. Mussel shell–tempered pottery continued to be made for five or six centuries, following which other types of pottery were made, ushering in what archaeologists call the Protohistoric period. Mussel shell–tempered pottery thus becomes a diagnostic of the Mississippi period. By this process, any archaeologist familiar with his or her area can look at a piece of pottery and immediately know the period to which it belongs. The same method works with

A.D., B.C., OR . . . ?

For a long time, it was traditional in archaeology to date artifacts, sites, and events by reference to the Christian calendar. For example, Christopher Columbus sailed the ocean blue in A.D. 1492, while the Sphinx in Egypt was built around 2500 B.C. A.D. is an abbreviation for *anno Domini* ("in the year of the Lord") and indicates that the event in question falls within the Christian era. B.C. is an abbreviation for "before Christ." It is still conventional to use these referents when communicating with a nonscientific audience, and indeed they continue to be used in many scientific publications, although the abbreviations C.E. and B.C.E. ("common era" and "before the common era") are sometimes substituted.

With the advent of radiocarbon dating, it became problematical to continue this practice in all scientific publications, as archaeology was being done in countries around the globe, and practitioners from every culture needed a common reference point for reporting their dates. The standard settled on is B.P., meaning "before the present." Ironically, this does not refer to the actual present, because that would involve a moving target. Instead, it refers to the year A.D. 1950, approximately when radiocarbon dating began. So a date of A.D. 1492 becomes 458 B.P., while 2500 B.C. becomes 4450 B.P. So, just remember that Columbus made a voyage great in four hundred fifty-eight, and you'll have it knocked!

CALIBRATING RADIOCARBON DATES

When physicist Willard Libby invented radiocarbon dating in the late 1940s, it was assumed that the amount of radioactive carbon in the atmosphere remained stable over time. This turns out not to be the case. The amount varies from year to year based on the earth's position in space and other factors. How did scientists discover this, and what can they do about the problem it presents for radiocarbon dating?

The answers and the solution are one and the same. The variation in atmospheric carbon was discovered by the ingeniously simple method of dating the individual, annual rings of living trees. Because trees grow from the outside, the inner wood dies as time passes,

preserving a yearly record of the atmospheric carbon balance. Scientists took cores from very old living trees and matched them up with old, dead trees in arid areas like the American Southwest. By radiocarbon-dating the individual rings, whose calendrical age is known by working backward from today, a carbon record has been assembled that shows the variation over the last several thousand years. Similar methods have been used with coral, which also grows in annual increments and lives for a very long time indeed. The resulting calibration curves are used to adjust radiocarbon dates so that they are more accurate.

points and some other artifacts. This is also why, if you collect arrowheads or other artifacts, it is *extremely* important to keep the stuff from any one spot separated from all other stuff: mix it up, and you are mixing up things from different sites and different periods, creating confusion that can never be undone.

Archaeologists can use artifact styles in another way, as well. At any one time, several different styles of any one kind of artifact might be produced. Think about

A prehistoric, mussel shell–tempered pot from a Mississippi-period site in Warren County. Shell-tempered pottery is considered to be a general diagnostic of the Mississippi period. Photo courtesy of the Mississippi Department of Archives and History.

all the different kinds of cars on the road today, for example. They all have the same function—to move us around—but there is a lot of variability in what the cars look like. Today there are lots of SUVs on the road; ten years ago there weren't that many, and ten years from now there will likely be either more or fewer of them. If we take collections of a particular artifact type—pottery, say—from several archaeological sites, and then divide those collections of pottery up into the different styles represented at each site, we can arrange the sites through time so that we see the different pottery styles appear, grow in popularity, and then decline until they disappear, just like cars, or clothes, or any other kind of artifact where style can be expressed appear, grow in popularity, and eventually disappear. This method of arranging artifact collections through time is called *seriation*. Some groundbreaking work using seriation was done in Mississippi in the 1930s and 1940s by an ingenious archaeologist named James Ford, who was a native of Water Valley. We are still building on his pioneering work today.

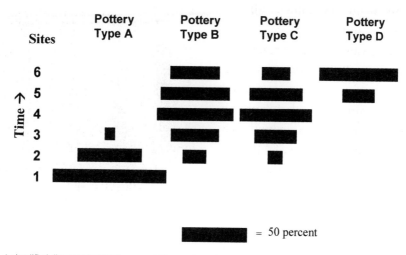

A simplified diagram showing how a seriation works to depict change through time in the relative proportions of different pottery styles.

Absolute dating methods are another kind of creature altogether. These are methods that actually tell you how old something is, within a range of error. The most famous is radiocarbon dating. Over the last twenty years, as I've given talks to various public groups around the state, I've been intrigued at how many people know about radiocarbon dating but don't know how it works. Here's a very simple explanation. Cosmic rays from space are constantly bombarding the earth. These strike the atmosphere, where they collide with various elements. The most common element in the atmosphere is nitrogen. When neutrons produced by a cosmic ray strike an atom of nitrogen, this can have the strange but entirely predictable effect of turning that atom into an isotope, or form, of carbon called carbon 14. Some isotopes of carbon, such as carbon 12 and carbon 13, are inherently stable. Carbon 14 is inherently unstable, meaning that it decays radioactively over time. Thanks to physics, we know how long it takes for unstable isotopes to decay.

Now, all the while that this is going on, plants are busy taking up carbon dioxide from the atmosphere as they photosynthesize. They take up all kinds of carbon, in the same relative amounts as are in the atmosphere. Animals that eat the plants likewise take up the same proportions of carbon 12, carbon 13, and carbon 14 into their bodies. And, guess what? As we eat plants and animals, *we also* take up these three forms of the same element. In your body, right now, radioactive isotopes are busily decaying away. But don't worry—the radiation won't hurt you, and as long as you continue eating, you will continue to replenish your supply.

Until you die, that is. At that point, you will, of course, quit taking in any elements at all. As long as any part of you is left, though, it will still have some carbon 12 and carbon 13 in it. It also has carbon 14, at least for about fifty thousand years, after which there is so little left that it can't be measured accurately. The point is that, because carbon 14 is decaying at a known rate, all you have to do is look at the ratio of it and the other carbon types left in the remains of any once-living thing, do a little math, and presto! You know approximately when that organism died. This method has been an enormous boon for archaeologists, because we often find the remains of lots of things that used to be alive—wood charcoal from a fire hearth, for instance, or discarded animal bones—at the sites where we work. As long as our site is no older than about fifty thousand years, and contains any sort of organic remains, we can get a radiocarbon date. Nowadays, very small samples can be dated; some scientists are even trying to date individual grains of pollen! The main limitation of the method is that it works only on organic remains. You cannot, therefore, radiocarbon-date a spear point or any other kind of stone tool, nor can you radiocarbon-date pottery clay, which would be nice to be able to do. If you find some pottery in a stratum at a site, along with some charcoal that can be radiocarbon-dated, can you be sure that the two things belong together? What if the pottery lay on the ground for a thousand years, then a forest fire came through and produced lots of charcoal that got into the soil around that pottery? Couldn't the radiocarbon date from that charcoal throw you off by a millennium?

You bet it could. That's why it's nice to have other dating methods. For pottery, a method growing in popularity is *thermoluminescence dating*. This is a really ingenious way to date things that have been heated, like a pot that has been fired at a high temperature, for example. The method works like this. Inside clay there are—here we go again—unstable isotopes of elements like uranium. As these decay, the freed particles go winging out into space. But not all of them! Some are caught within the molecular structure of the clay itself, like insects trapped in a minuscule web. If the clay is heated to a sufficient temperature, the traps open and those particles are finally freed. So if you make a pot and fire it, you release all the particles that had built up in the clay as stored energy. As the pot cools, the process starts over as the clay begins to trap particles again, creating a new supply of stored energy. Now, if you take that same pot hundreds or thousands of years later—or even a small sherd from it—and reheat it to its original firing temperature, the stored energy is released in a brief burst of light! The intensity of the light can be measured and the amount of stored energy calculated. Because the isotopes decay at a known rate, and because we know about what proportion of them get caught in traps, we can again do some math and tell how long ago the pot was originally fired. This same method can be used on rocks if they have been heated. As it happens, Native Americans heated rocks for thousands of years in Mississippi, as heat-treating makes the tough gravel that was often used for stone tools much easier to work. So every flake, stone tool, and potsherd that was ever heated, from every Native American site in the state—literally billions of artifacts—can potentially be dated via thermoluminescence.

Yet another absolute method is *archaeomagnetism*. The earth's magnetic field wobbles back and forth over time. If sediments are sufficiently heated, tiny magnetic particles within those sediments that are lined up on north like so many compass needles become stuck. Geophysicists working with deep-sea cores have compiled a record of magnetic variation over time. At an archaeological site, sediments are frequently heated, as happens, for example, with a clay fire hearth. With care, the hearth itself can be sampled so that the "frozen" magnetic alignment of its particles can be recorded. This alignment is compared to the master record, providing us with a date for when the hearth was used.

There are many other absolute dating methods, some of which work in temperate woodland settings like Mississippi, some of which are more applicable in places like East Africa where the archaeological record goes back millions of years. Just to list a few, they are: potassium-argon dating, argon-argon dating, fluoride dating, uranium-series dating, dendrochronology or tree-ring dating, obsidian hydration dating, oxidizable carbon ratio dating, lichen dating—and the list goes on. And new methods are still being invented. These are the tools with which we do our jobs. Like wizards, we work with the stuff of time. And once time has been controlled for—well, then the questions get interesting. For then we can attempt to do what no other discipline can do: we can explore what it means to be human over the long term.

DATING BUILDINGS WITH BRICKS

Archaeologists in Mississippi often find evidence of old houses at Historic-period sites. For example, a low pile of bricks might mark where a chimney once stood. The artifacts from the site might give you a general age—late nineteenth to early twentieth century, say—but is there any way to get a more accurate date from the building remains themselves?

There is, as it turns out, at least in some cases. In the early nineteenth century, the manufacture of bricks was pretty much a cottage industry. If you needed a batch of bricks for your house foundation or a chimney, you might dig the clay nearby, make some wooden molds, and shape and bake the bricks yourself. Eventually, the industry became more formalized as commercial brick and tile companies began to exploit the rich clay beds of Mississippi. This led to the standardization of bricks, which generally got smaller and more uniform through time.

Archaeologists can use this fact to get a fairly accurate date for many old buildings in the state, by constructing what is called a brick index.

Archaeologist Jack Elliott devised a brick index for the "Golden Triangle" region of north Mississippi—the area including the cities of Starkville, Columbus, and West Point. He did this by going to buildings on the campus of Mississippi State University and measuring a sample of bricks from each. He used buildings with cornerstones so that the date of construction was known. As expected, bricks in the MSU buildings get smaller and less variable in size through time. Jack discovered that the method works best for older buildings. By about 1905, bricks become too similar in size for them to be readily discriminated. But if you have several old buildings in your town, you might be able to make an index of your own, which you can use to date other buildings whose age is unknown.

An old brick (left) and a modern brick (right), showing how brick sizes have changed through time.

DID YOU FIND
ANY GOLD YET?

Public interest in archaeology is generally fed by slick, high-quality production efforts like *National Geographic* or the Discovery Channel. Such outlets perform a valuable service in letting people know what is going on in the world of archaeology. Unfortunately, they tend to focus on the spectacular, leading many people to believe that archaeology is nothing but a kind of glorified tomb robbing, a la Indiana Jones. This is a very unhealthy misconception. If you watch the Indiana Jones movies carefully, you will discover that the only ones doing any decent archaeology are the Germans.

There is another lingering misperception that has led to a lot of destruction in Mississippi and elsewhere: the idea that gold, or jewels, or some other kind of treasure is buried in Indian mounds. I have visited many, many mounds in our state and have very rarely seen one that didn't have an old "pot hole" on top, compliments of some thoughtless individual who dug into a monument that may have stood there undisturbed for two thousand years or more. And, of course, such treasure seekers do not find any "treasure" in the mounds—the prehistoric Indians of Mississippi did not smelt metals like gold or silver. Very, very

A copper ear spool from the Bynum Mounds site in Chickasaw County. Photo courtesy of the Mississippi Department of Archives and History.

rarely mounds might contain artifacts of copper, raw nuggets of which were beaten into sheet form and then cut or shaped into ornaments like "ear spools," artifacts that look a lot like yo-yos but which were inserted into the ear lobe for aesthetic purposes. Copper also was used to cover wood or cane to make a kind of musical instrument called a pan-pipe. Such artifacts do not hold an inherent value like gold does; there is, at most, a few pennies' worth of copper in a single ear spool. Far more valuable, and what is being lost when someone carelessly goes digging into mounds or any other kind of site, is the scientific knowledge that such artifacts can yield. Copper, for example, does not occur naturally in Mississippi; its presence at prehistoric sites is therefore direct evidence of extensive trade networks that spanned much of the continent thousands of years before Europeans ever landed on American shores. How will we ever figure out the nature and extent of those past trade networks if the objects of trade are ripped from their contexts? If you are an artifact collector, please—confine your activities to the surface! You should *never* dig, for if you do, you will inadvertently destroy evidence that is invisible without a trained eye. If you are interested in archaeology—which you must be if you collect artifacts—then why destroy the very object of your interest?

Particularly damaging are those people who dig into sites knowing full well what they are after: pots, points, or other artifacts that can be sold to collectors or dealers in antiquities. There is an international market for such things, and it has fueled the destruction of sites across the globe. Mississippi is no exception—artifacts from our state reside in private collections all around the world. It is possible to go to Japan, for example, and find pots that were looted out of burial mounds in Mississippi. When those artifacts are stolen from their sites, an irreplaceable part of Mississippi's cultural heritage is destroyed. And for what? To satisfy the insatiable appetite of some wealthy curio collector. *Such activities are, in many cases, against the law.*

Why? Well, think about it. Native Americans did not just throw away whole pots or other elaborate artifacts, which took a considerable amount of labor and expertise to produce. Such objects are almost always found in only one context: as grave goods accompanying human burials. So when you see whole pots or other artifacts for sale down at the flea market, it's a good bet that they were dug up out of someone's grave. That's *not* OK. The same laws that say it's illegal to go out and dig up your city cemetery say that it's illegal to knowingly disturb *any* human burial, Indian or otherwise. Bizarrely enough, it took a ruling from the state attorney general to settle whether or not the law applied to burials at Native American archaeological sites—in essence, to say that Indians are people, too! To this day I still encounter people who do not get this basic idea. More than once I have tried to convince landowners that it's not a good idea to land-level a site, for example, because there may be people buried there. "It's just Indian stuff" is often the reply. One landowner bluntly informed me that, in his opinion, anyone who cared about such things was a fool. Such a callous disregard for our common humanity is so mind-boggling that it is difficult to know how to deal with it, other than pointing out, as often as possible, that *it is against the law to disturb graves, including Native American graves.* Which you might hit if you are out digging for artifacts. So don't!

How is it, then, that archaeologists are allowed to excavate burials? Before I answer that question, there is another misconception that needs to be laid to rest: namely, that archaeologists intentionally seek out burials when they dig. There was a time when this was true. Decades ago, part of the mission of archaeologists working for the state was to find artifacts to put on display at the state museum. In some countries, there still is a focus on tombs. I believe it is safe to say that such is generally not the case in the United States anymore, and with good reason. Many American Indians, descendants of those brave people who managed to survive the brutal clash of cultures that began when Christopher Columbus first set foot on a tiny island in the Bahamas, are rightly concerned about having the graves of their ancestors dug up. Most archaeologists that I know are quite sensitive to this issue, so much so that it was with the support of the archaeological community that NAGPRA (the *Native American Graves Protection and Repatriation Act*) was passed into law in 1990 (this law will be discussed further in chapter 11). Especially in those cases where an archaeological site can be linked to a known tribe, archaeologists are careful to consult with Native Americans prior to beginning an excavation. Indeed, when taxpayers' money is involved, such consultation is required under the law. Of course, it only makes sense for archaeologists and Native Americans to work together, as both are ultimately interested in the same things: exploring and appreciating the rich cultural diversity of Native American societies as they existed—and still exist!—in North America, and trying to preserve that legacy for future generations.

This is not to say that archaeologists don't dig burials: we do, when the situation demands it. Imagine, for example, that a new highway is being built through Mississippi. That highway would be certain to destroy many archaeological sites, and if burials exist at those sites, they, too, would be destroyed unless something was done about it. Archaeologists hired to mitigate the impacts of construction in Mississippi must obtain a special permit from the state that allows them to excavate burials in this sort of salvage situation. Not just Native American burials, either, but any human burials that are in the impact zone. We are the specialists who are trained to conduct such work. It is conducted with great technical skill and with due respect for the individuals being exhumed. It is done in consultation with Native Americans or the representatives of other ethnic groups as appropriate. And if the remains can be shown to be culturally affiliated—that is, if they can be linked to any particular Native American group today—then they may be passed to that group once the archaeological work is done, if such a request is made. Once they have been thus *repatriated,* the remains become the responsibility of the Native Americans themselves, who may rebury them or do whatever they feel is necessary and right. This sea change in how archaeology is practiced has, by and large, been a positive development. There are, of course, still people on both sides of the fence who are strongly opposed to compromise of any kind: Native Americans who feel that no archaeologist should ever dig at any site again, archaeologists who feel that the scientific value of the archaeological record outweighs all other considerations. As with most political situations, the way forward lies somewhere in the middle. Archaeologists and Native Americans all should feel justifiably proud of what has been accomplished in the last decade. I hope that we can continue to work together as allies, to learn from one another, and to more effectively address the problems of site destruction and looting that continue to this day.

But back to gold. The most amusing story I have heard concerning archaeology and gold came from an archaeologist whom I met in Israel. This fellow had worked at a very large and famous site there called Gezer, where he actually had discovered gold—a cache of beautiful jewelry left behind and forgotten over three thousand years ago. As he told me this story, he proudly brandished his "magic trowel," the same instrument that he had been wielding when the golden artifacts had been found. I was suitably impressed. A few days later we were working out in the hot, Near Eastern sun when I couldn't help but notice that he had the most hangdog expression on his face. Concerned, I asked him what the problem was. Sheepishly, he confessed that he had gone to visit the *bet shimush* (pronounced "bait-she-moosh," accent on "bait" and "moosh"—literally, Hebrew for "house of use"; an outhouse would be a fair description of the rather primitive facilities at the site where we were working). As my acquaintance was straightening up, his business having been conducted, the "magic trowel" slipped from his belt and plunged into the odoriferous darkness below. He was so crestfallen that I didn't have the heart to ask him if he thought that it had struck gold. I can only imagine what sort of interpretations future archaeologists will make when they excavate the trowel thousands of years from now.

In answer to the question posed in the title of this chapter, the answer is "yes." I myself *did* find gold once, in the most unlikely of places. During my Forest Service days I conducted a survey of a proposed timber sale area in the hills of Marshall County. One morning my technician and I spotted a site on the gentle slope of a pine-covered hill. It was easy to detect even without putting a shovel in the ground, as beneath the pines there were privet, yucca, daffodils, roses, and other plants that signified an old house place as surely as if someone had set out the welcome mat. According to standard practice, we began digging shovel tests across the site to obtain a sample of artifacts and to see what kind of shape it was in. The shape was pretty bad, as it happens. It was a house site, all right, one that dated to the early 1900s based on the nails, glass, ceramics, and other artifacts we recovered. It had been severely eroded at some time in the past, and really contained nothing of scientific or historical interest. But I remember it well, out of the hundreds of such sites that I recorded over the years, because of what I found in one shovel test. I kicked the shovel into the hard ground, hefted the dirt into my screen, and had begun to work it through when I caught the unmistakable glint of gold. Unlike most metals, gold does not lose its luster while in the ground: it still has that legendary shine no matter how long it has been buried (in this case, about sixty or seventy years). I freely confess that I felt a special thrill as I reached into the screen and picked up a tiny ring, one that obviously was meant for a child. At the top of the ring were two small, interlocking hearts. I could imagine a little girl losing this precious possession back during the Great Depression, and then having to go into the small cabin where she lived and confess with weeping eyes her loss to her parents. I wish that I had a time machine so that I could go back and return the small treasure that, against all odds, I was lucky enough to rediscover so many years later.

WHO WERE THEY?

The only answer I can give to an embarrassingly large number of questions I am frequently asked is "We don't really know." One of the most common of these, usually asked after I have finished talking about excavations at a particular site, is "What tribe were they?" People are curious about who left all this stuff behind. Were they Choctaw? Chickasaw? Some other tribe? The impulse behind this question is perfectly understandable. People want to work from the known to the unknown, to have some anchor upon which to secure their ship of inquiry. Although I sympathize with the inclination, I realized long ago that to do archaeology in such a way that we actually learn something, rather than just telling ourselves stories, we are obliged to raise the anchor and sail into uncharted waters. After all, the "known"—that is, historical time—is only the briefest glimpse of what has transpired during the course of human cultural development. To try to understand everything that came before only by reference to what we see now is like trying to establish the plot of a movie by looking at the last frame in a reel of film.

Nothing is more telling in this regard than is trying to assign ethnicity to artifacts. Unless we are working with Historic-era artifacts, we usually are *not* dealing with the known, in any sense. We are dealing very much with the unknown. We put names to the vast span of time that is prehistory—the Paleo-Indian period, the Archaic period, the Woodland, the Mississippian, the Protohistoric—but we cannot put back the names that the Native American peoples themselves would have used, for we do not, and cannot, know them. The ancestors of the historically known tribes did not have written languages, so there is no historical record to access. And while oral tradition can convey some interesting information, it is essentially a contemporary body of knowledge, continually shaped by generations of storytellers to convey matters of principle and value, not necessarily historical fact. The oral—and even the written—traditions of more recent migrants to these shores are only a few hundred years old, and yet they contain little that can be taken at face value as "fact." Did George Washington really chop down a cherry tree? No. But it makes a great tale with which we can instruct our children about the virtues of truthfulness. Oral history and science are two different things, each of which can contribute to the other, but neither of which necessarily conveys truth with a capital "T."

In general terms, southeastern archaeologists divide the last fourteen thousand years up into the following periods: Paleo-Indian, Early Archaic, Middle Archaic, Late Archaic, Early Woodland/Gulf Formational, Middle Woodland, Late Woodland, Mississippi, and Protohistoric. I will describe some of the characteristics that we believe typify what life was like in these periods. But it is important to realize two things. First of all, these divisions are arbitrary creations of the archaeologists: they are not "real" in the sense of self-recognized ethnic groups or past political or social boundaries. Secondly, we have only just begun to explore and understand the archaeological record of Mississippi: every year brings something new. So everything that we think we know is most certainly subject to change.

The *Paleo-Indian period* began about fourteen thousand years ago, when the first people arrived in Mississippi. It was a much different

TODAY	
A.D. 1700	Historic
A.D. 1500	Protohistoric
	Mississippi
A.D. 1000	
	Late Woodland
A.D. 600	
	Middle Woodland
A.D. 0	
	Early Woodland/ Gulf Formational
1000 B.C.	
	Late Archaic
3000 B.C.	
	Middle Archaic
5000 B.C.	
	Early Archaic
7000 B.C.	
	Paleo-Indian
12000 B.C.	

place then, with spruce trees, elephants, and other strange plants and animals. The elephants were *mastodons*, hairy creatures that browsed the forests of the Southeast feeding on leaves and other tough forage. It is possible that the first Native Americans in what is now Mississippi hunted these animals, although we have no direct evidence of it. We know, in fact, very, very little about these first cultures in the state, other than the fact that they made exquisitely beautiful spear points. We call these point types Clovis, Cumberland, Beaver Lake, Quad, and other names. We also know about some of their other tools— steeply flaked stone *end scrapers*, for example. But intact Paleo-Indian sites are rare, and we have much to learn about life in Mississippi so long ago.

Following the Paleo-Indian comes the *Archaic*, traditionally broken down into Early, Middle, and Late periods. *Early Archaic*, a period that stretches from nine thousand to seven thousand years ago, also

A generalized culture-history chart for Mississippi. The period boundaries might change depending upon what artifacts are considered to be diagnostic. For example, some archaeologists might move the lower boundary of the Early Archaic period back in time one to two thousand years to encompass the "Dalton culture," which other archaeologists consider to be "late Paleo-Indian." It is important to remember that these lines are an arbitrary creation of the archaeologists; they simply provide a shorthand way to discuss what happened during different spans of time in the past.

is very poorly known. The world was a changing place, as new forests and attendant plant and animal species came to inhabit the warming landscape. Spear points became much smaller, perhaps indicative of a new emphasis on smaller animals such as deer (the mastodon, alas, had become extinct). Such points typically are notched on either side, and often are ground smooth along the base, a trait that initially appeared during the Paleo-Indian period. Presumably, this basal grinding had something to do with lashing a point onto a spear shaft in such a way that the lashing wouldn't be cut by sharp stone edges. If you find a point with basal grinding, you can pretty much bet that it's Early Archaic or older.

A Paleo-Indian Clovis point from near Grenada. Photo courtesy of the Mississippi Department of Archives and History.

Middle Archaic, the period from about seven thousand to five thousand years ago, is turning out to be one of the most interesting parts of prehistory in Mississippi. The climate became warmer and drier, a fluctuation in temperature and precipitation known as the *Hypsithermal*. It was not that different from today—on average, perhaps one to three degrees hotter every summer—but coincident with this relatively minor climatic change came massive cultural changes. Sites with *midden*—

WHAT DID THE PREHISTORIC INDIANS EAT?

If you want to know what makes another culture tick, find out what it puts in its collective stomach. This is an excuse I use whenever I am traveling abroad. "This is for research purposes," I say between mouthfuls, and pass the plate for more data. Much of the way in which any culture is organized is directly related to how the members of that culture obtain, process, store, distribute, prepare, and consume food. As the "shopper-gatherers" of today, for example, we are tied to the supermarket for food and the utility companies for power. (And to the fire department, when we get a little overzealous with the starter fluid on grilling days.)

It is therefore of great interest to archaeologists to find out what people ate in the past. This is done through the recovery of plant and animal remains from archaeological sites. Sometimes such remains can be remarkably well preserved, giving us a direct window onto past peoples' daily lives. Not surprisingly, the prehistoric Indians of Mississippi ate a lot of the same game animals we hunt today: white-tailed deer, turkeys, gray and fox squirrels, rabbits, raccoons, catfish, drum, and other fish—the list is a long one. Probably longer than you would imagine, for a lot of animals were eaten that are not standard fare today, such as freshwater mussels and snails, box tortoises, and several species of snake. Bioarchaeologists compare the bones from archaeological sites to bones from modern specimens to identify the kinds of animals eaten in the past. Material evidence related to Indian hunting and gathering practices include spear and arrow points, worked flakes used as butchering tools, and wooden fish weirs placed in streams to trap fish. We also know that they had dogs, as we find dog skeletons buried at prehistoric sites, and it is likely that those dogs were used for hunting.

The Indians of Mississippi became farmers beginning about one thousand years ago, raising various crops of which maize, squash, and beans were the most important. Even while they were farmers they continued to hunt and fish, taking advantage of Mississippi's rich environment and prospering for centuries before the coming of the Europeans changed their societies forever. This tradition of a mixed farming and hunting economy still characterizes life in much of rural Mississippi today.

A prehistoric site in Lowndes County seen from the air. The site is marked by a midden, a dark, organic-rich soil developed at long-term human settlements. Note the house in the woods at right for scale. Photo courtesy of Janet Rafferty.

Middle Archaic–period Benton points from Union, Pontotoc, and Lee counties.

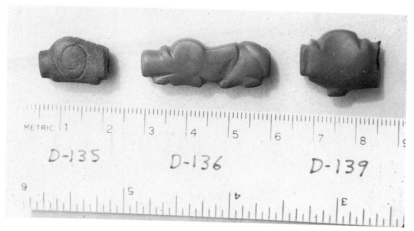

Stylized stone beads from the Middle Archaic–period Denton site in Quitman County. Photo courtesy of the Mississippi Department of Archives and History.

deep, dark, organically enriched soil produced by intensive human occupation—appeared in abundance. Hickory trees apparently thrived in the drier conditions, and excavations at Middle Archaic sites across the Southeast have produced pits absolutely chock full of charred hickory-nut shells. Raw materials from distant sources began to flow into Mississippi in astonishing amounts. Middle Archaic Benton points, for example, are overwhelmingly made out of a kind of gray rock called Fort Payne chert that was obtained in the Tennessee River valley. Pebbles of red jasper were polished and drilled into tubular beads. Stone bead making, in fact, appears to have been a specialty of Middle Archaic people, and southwest Mississippi seems to have been the center of the industry. Frequently, the beads take the stylized shapes of big-eyed creatures whose nature is hard to determine: they may be insects, or birds, or some mythical combination of animals that speaks to us of a long-lost cosmology. There is much that we don't know about the Middle Archaic, but the extraordinary finds coming out of Mississippi are causing many archaeologists to begin to focus on this intriguing part of the past.

Freshwater mussels from a prehistoric site in Coahoma County. These animals were an important food source for Indians for thousands of years.

Late Archaic, the period from about five thousand to three thousand years ago, provides a telling lesson of how far we still have to go in Mississippi archaeology. We know precious little about what went on during those two thousand years. Part of the problem is that there are no really distinctive artifact styles that typify the period. Pottery wasn't introduced until right at the very end (the first pots were actually carved out of sandstone or a kind of soft rock called *soapstone*—ceramic ones came slightly later), and Late Archaic spear points are nondescript, stemmed forms that lasted without major change up until about A.D. 600, when the bow and arrow was introduced. Because the artifacts aren't that distinctive, archaeologists have a hard time even knowing for sure when the Late Archaic period is represented at a site. The tendency is to call sites with stemmed points but no pottery Late Archaic, but arguing from negative evidence is always risky. In essence, the period seems to be one during which a generalized hunting and gathering existence took place against a temperate woodland environmental backdrop. Freshwater mussels apparently increased in importance as a food source, with many large *shell mounds* accumulating on the rivers of the Southeast. These shell mounds have been a focus of *pothunters*—people who loot sites—for a long time, because the shell neutralizes soil acids so that artifacts of bone and other perishable materials are fortuitously preserved. I have heard horror stories about people hauling pumps out to shell mounds on their johnboats and literally blasting the sites away with powerful jets of river water while they scanned the melting debris for projectile points or other artifacts. What a pity, that something of such antiquity and importance can be destroyed in a matter of minutes to satisfy someone's greed.

Following the Late Archaic comes either the *Early Woodland* or the *Gulf Formational* period, depending on where you are in the state and to whose scenario you subscribe. The names don't really matter that much, as they are simply creations that archaeologists use to communicate with one another. But what happened between about three thousand and two thousand years ago matters quite a lot, because people's lives began to change in substantial and profound ways. There is good evidence to suggest that during this time people became *sedentary*, which is to say that they quit moving about the landscape in a seasonal hunt for resources and settled down to live in one place throughout the year. Why is this change such an important one? Well, lots of interesting things seem to happen when people settle down. For one thing, populations tend to increase dramatically. It's no longer necessary to have wide spacing between births, as you don't have to carry small children around the landscape. If you commit to living in one place, your architecture has to become more substantial to last throughout the different seasons. You begin to put much more pressure on the local environment. This last is not something that we generally think about where

MEASURING PREHISTORIC HUMAN ENVIRONMENTAL IMPACT

A popular myth in American culture holds that Indians were "natural conservationists" who never took more than they needed from the natural world, that they existed in enviable harmony with the environments in which they lived. Scientists in geography, ecology, and other disciplines who refer to the landscapes of America before Columbus's arrival as "presettlement" ecosystems have bolstered this myth. Presettlement! As though fourteen thousand years of human habitation had no measurable effect on the land! Not only is this idea erroneous, but it also does a disservice to American Indian cultures by treating them as though they were invisible. It is safe to assume that the prehistoric inhabitants of Mississippi changed the landscapes they inhabited, consciously and unconsciously. But how do we move beyond mere assumptions to actually detect and measure the amount of that change?

As with most forms of evidence in archaeology, we dig it up. In an earlier sidebar, I described how we analyze pollen, snail shells, and the remains of other forms of life to understand what the environment looked like in the past. If we detect changes in those remains over time, we may be looking at the effects of human actions on the landscape. For example, a sudden increase in the amount of ragweed pollen is a pretty good indication that a lot of trees were being cut down (go to a piece of land that was recently clearcut and you'll see lots of ragweed growing in the disturbed ground). A change from shade-loving to open-ground snails would be a similar indicator. We also have good historical evidence related to how Indians managed the landscape. For example, there are accounts from across North America of how Indians regularly set fires to keep down undergrowth and to promote the growth of plants that were attractive to game animals.

Measuring the scale of prehistoric human impact in North America is something we are only just now beginning to grapple with. For my doctoral thesis at the University of Sheffield, England, I studied the remains of freshwater mussels from shell midden sites over a large part of the southeastern United States. Many species of mussel are today either extinct or on the verge of extinction. Biologists attribute this decline to water pollution, among other things. The only real form of water pollution in prehistoric times was siltation, the washing of soil from disturbed land into rivers and streams. When I examined the prehistoric mussel remains, I found that the species known to be most sensitive to pollution today began to decline in numbers as much as five thousand years ago, and that the rate of decline increased as Indians in the region adopted agriculture as a way of life. This appears to be a measurable effect of erosion resulting from Indian land use. So the pattern of past environmental impact is similar to one we see today, although the degree and rate of that impact increased enormously in historic times with the advent of modern land-use practices. We still have a lot to learn about how past human actions changed the world, and there doubtless are lessons to be learned about how we can better manage our lands today.

Native Americans are concerned, but it certainly bears consideration. Have you ever been to a campground and tried to find fallen branches with which to start a fire? Hard to do, isn't it? Because everyone else has had the same idea, and all the branches are gone. Some sites in Mississippi were occupied more or less continuously for two to three thousand years, or even longer. How hard do you think it would be to find fuel wood in that kind of situation? Especially when fires had to be burning pretty much all the time for cooking, meat smoking, mosquito control, heat, light, and who knows how many other things. Add to this the wood needed for house construction, canoes, spear shafts, axe handles, and so on, and you begin to understand how a sedentary lifestyle can transform the landscape around a site.

Another thing that begins to happen with sedentariness is that, because you are no longer moving to all the resources, you have to bring

Gulf Formational–period pottery sherds from a prehistoric site in Lowndes County. Photo courtesy of Janet Rafferty.

all the resources to you. This means trade. It also means that you must develop good storage facilities to preserve enough food to get you through the lean winter months. It is no accident that this is the time when pottery first becomes widespread—not only can you cook with it, but also you can store food in it for a long time. Your choice of living location also must be a careful one: close enough to permanent water so that you don't suffer from its lack, far enough away or high enough up so that your house doesn't wash away if a flood comes. Put all of these

An elaborately decorated Middle Woodland–period pottery sherd from Union County. Photo courtesy of Janet Rafferty.

things together, and you can see why archaeologists are so interested in knowing when and why people made this dramatic transition in lifestyle.

The *Middle Woodland* period lasted from about two thousand to fourteen hundred years ago, a time during which conical burial mounds began to be built. These are discussed in detail in the next chapter, so I won't elaborate here except to say that where thousands once existed in Mississippi, only a few hundred, at most, are left. Most have been lost to land leveling, construction, pothunters, erosion, and other destructive forces, which is too bad, because the people building those mounds were up to a lot of interesting things. Trade increased, with exotic raw materials coming into Mississippi from far away. Peculiar art styles appeared on pottery, such as concentric "bull's-eye" patterns and depictions of large-beaked birds with long, curved necks. Mounds were built all over the Eastern Woodlands of North America at about this time, an indication that Native American societies were not independent groups living in isolation but were active players on the stage of the world as they knew it. The famous Bynum and Pharr mound sites on the Natchez Trace Parkway date to the Middle Woodland period.

The *Late Woodland* period, which lasted from about fourteen hundred to a thousand years ago, was a very dynamic and active time. One of the most important things that happened in what is now Mississippi was the introduction of the bow and arrow around A.D. 600. Can you imagine what a change that must have been? Hunting and warfare must have taken on whole new dimensions. Certainly warfare existed, as evidenced by human skeletons with clear indications of violence (see chapter 8 for a description of one such burial). What was driving such warfare? It may have been competition for resources. Dr. Patricia Galloway conducted a study of the records at the Mississippi Department of Archives and History and found that, of all the prehistoric sites that have been recorded in Mississippi, there are more from the Late Woodland period than from any other time. And Late Woodland sites are everywhere: in the valleys, in the hills, in the deltas, in the prairies—everywhere. As far as we know, people in Mississippi at the time were still hunter-gatherers, albeit sedentary ones. It is possible that pressure on the environment had mounted to the point that, given the available technology, people had begun to push the carrying capacity of the land.

Burial mounds were not commonly built during the Late Woodland period; rather, the dead were generally folded up into what archaeologists call a "semiflexed" position and buried in simple holes in the ground. There are very few grave goods found with such burials, although occasionally a large, broken piece of pottery was placed under the deceased's head. Based on the animal bones and plant remains recovered at sites, people were eating pretty much anything that they could get their hands on: box turtles, for example, and river snails, and freshwater mussels no bigger than your thumbnail. Evidence suggests that people were constrained, possibly by population pressure, to use only the environment immediately around their villages. The Late Woodland period is definitely a piece of prehistory that we need to know more about.

The *Mississippi* period (sometimes called the Mississippian period) comes next in time. It is named for the river, and indeed Mississippian cultures have been described as riverine cultures. A lot was going on between about one thousand and five hundred years ago that makes Mississippian the most extensively studied prehistoric period in eastern North America. For a start, people of the time were farmers, growing corn, squash, beans, sunflowers, amaranth, and other crops. Like farmers today, they were attracted to fertile, well-drained soils. Scattered "farmstead" sites dot the landscape in some parts of Mississippi; these small, presumably single-family dwellings were no doubt tied to the occasional mound centers found up and down the river valleys. For mound building had begun again, but in a different fashion from that practiced by Middle Woodland peoples. It was not common practice for mounds of dirt to be piled up to bury the dead. Rather, flat *platform mounds* were built upon which buildings were erected. In these buildings lived people of prominence and power, the secular and religious leaders of society. Palisades often surrounded mound sites: these defensive walls were made of wooden posts set side by side in the ground and often had protruding bastions from which archers could throw down a lethal crossfire upon attacking foes. The posts were usually set in *wall trenches*, narrow ditches laboriously dug with sharpened sticks and other tools. Wall trenches also were used in the construction of houses and other buildings. The site of Winterville, near Greenville, is an excellent example of a Mississippian mound center that is open to tourists.

A palisade trench at the Lyon's Bluff site, Oktibbeha County, under excavation. The narrow ditch was dug to insert wooden posts for a protective wall. Dark, circular stains in the center of the trench mark where posts once stood.

Wall trench houses and associated pit features being excavated at a Mississippi-period site in Tunica County. Photo courtesy of the Mississippi Department of Archives and History.

The extraordinary Emerald Mound near Natchez is another. If you've never seen that enormous mound, be prepared to have your breath taken away when you visit. Mounds will be further discussed in the next chapter.

Mississippian culture also is important because it was in operation when the first Europeans entered the interior of what is now Mississippi. This was the expedition of *Hernando de Soto*, a ruthless Spanish conquistador who was exploring for gold or other resources that would bring him fame and fortune back home. He knew his business, having been with Pizarro during the brutal conquest of the Inca in South America. We can only wonder what the native peoples thought upon seeing white men, horses, pigs, armor, metal bells,

A Soto-era "Clarksdale bell" from a contact-period Indian site in Coahoma County. Photo courtesy of John Connaway.

glass beads, and other strange objects for the first time. Soto failed in his endeavor—as discussed in the previous chapter, the southeastern Indians didn't have gold—but he left a trail of destruction in his wake. Some of the destruction came from the visible elements of the Spanish expedition: guns, lances, swords, war horses, war dogs—things that bewildered the Indians, who had never fought people like the Spaniards

A red-and-white painted water bottle from a Protohistoric-period site in Oktibbeha County. Photo courtesy of Janet Rafferty.

before. More destructive in the long run were the invisible elements, diseases to which Native Americans had no natural resistance that were carried by members of the Spanish force. Imagine what would happen if, within the next month, eighty percent of the people in your community died from a sickness that no one had seen before, a sickness that left the face and body cruelly marked with hot, red blotches. Such was smallpox. Other diseases—influenza, whooping cough, measles, mumps, typhoid fever, yellow fever, scarlet fever, bubonic plague—also ran rampant through Native American populations. In the centuries following Soto's travels through Mississippi in 1540–1541, an unknown number of Indians perished from these terrible, microscopic invaders.

Not coincidentally, the period between that first, fleeting contact with Europeans and later, sustained interaction between Old World and New World cultures—the period between about five hundred and three hundred years ago—was one of massive change. Archaeologists call this the *Protohistoric* period. And it is a very hazy time indeed. Entire settlements were abandoned while new ones formed from the remnants of once-powerful groups. New art styles arose and spread across large areas of the Southeast. Other traits appeared that had no precedent, such as burying the bodies of infants and small children—or the gathered bones of adults—in large ceramic jars that archaeologists call *burial urns*. Traditional knowledge built up over centuries had to rapidly evolve as people adjusted to the fact that other cultures, other lands, other materials, were part of creation. The archaeological record of the Protohistoric period is not an easy one to deal with, precisely because so much change took place in so short a time. A great deal of work remains to be done to bring light to that shadowy corner of Mississippi's past.

A mid-1800s daguerreotype of a young Choctaw man. Photo courtesy of Ken Carleton.

The *Historic* period proper begins, in Mississippi, with the eighteenth-century establishment of the French in the Natchez region, and continues today. The remains of Choctaw homesteads, Chickasaw villages, and settlements of other known Mississippi tribes—the Natchez, the Acolapissas, the Pascagoulas, the Yazoos, the Tunicas, the Biloxis, the Chakchiumas, and others—can still be found at archaeological sites around the state. It is important to note, however, that archaeologists do not confine themselves solely to Native American sites. There is an enormous amount to be learned about Historic-era cultures in Mississippi, be they Native American, European American, or African American, which simply cannot be learned from the written record. Dr. Amy Young, of the University of Southern Mississippi, has supervised digs at the locations of slave quarters at antebellum plantation sites, for example, and has found compelling evidence that slaves kept guns for hunting. Slaves with guns—the last thing in the world that someone conversant with southern antebellum history might expect.

Most of what we know about the institution of slavery in the Old South comes to us today from history books. But history is hampered by various biases: who wrote it, when, and, most importantly, why? While there are numerous historical sources relating to the everyday life of plantation owners, reliable accounts of slave life are harder to come by. What can archaeology tell us about this divisive chapter in Mississippi's history?

A lot, as it turns out. Dr. Amy Young of the University of Southern Mississippi is a historical archaeologist specializing in the antebellum South. She and her students conducted fieldwork at Saragossa Plantation, near Natchez. In addition to conducting standard archaeological excavations at the site of slave quarters, they also interviewed members of the nearby community of Saragossa who are descended from the plantation slaves. Dr.

Young and archaeologists Michael Tuma and Cliff Jenkins studied how slaves used hunting to counter risks in their daily lives. The bones of many types of wild animals were found where a slave cabin had stood, including deer, turtles, rabbits, squirrels, opossums, raccoons, gar, geese, and catfish. Although domesticated animals such as cattle, pigs, and chickens also were represented in the animal bones, hunting clearly was an important part of slave life at Saragossa Plantation. In addition to providing food, it likely offered a way to indoctrinate new members of the slave community, allowed men to have a "breadwinner" role even in the circumstances of slavery, and acted overall as a cohesive social bond for people who had little control over their destinies. Many of these aspects of hunting still exist in the descendent community at Saragossa today.

A slave cabin at the Saragossa Plantation near Natchez. Photo courtesy of Amy Young.

Even a relatively recent site, like the spot where a sharecropper's cabin stood in the 1930s, can tell us things about life during the Great Depression that we don't know or that have been forgotten. History doesn't write about the everyday folk of the world, even though their unwritten stories are really what life is all about. I have walked through the national forests of north Mississippi and spotted, with my archaeologist's eye, many subtle remains from that bygone era: piles of sandstone where crude chimneys once stood; circular depressions marking the locations of sunken-in cisterns; ragged patches of ornamental flowers that once graced the front yard of a poor but proud family; rectangular depressions revealing the unmarked graves of forgotten men, women, and children. Now, all is forest. It never fails to astonish me how, in just one generation, life in Mississippi changed so radically. The denizens of those innumerable house sites had no running water, no electricity. They had families that were amazingly large by today's standards—ten, twelve, fourteen children. Why? To keep one in one's old age, to provide labor to work the land, and to insure a family because so many infants died in those days when formal medical attention was hard to come by. Small tombstones are mute but poignant testimony to the high childhood mortality of the times. People worked desperately hard to farm the land with mule and plow, to fell trees to haul to the nearest sawmill with oxen, to try to accumulate enough money to someday actually own a place of their own. Very few achieved that dream, but their struggles are a part of Mississippi's legacy that should never be forgotten. And the material remains of that legacy should be preserved. When a people destroy their past, it speaks little for the kind of future that their own children will someday inherit.

DO I HAVE A MOUND
ON MY PLACE?

Many, many people have told me over the years about
"mounds" where they have collected lots of artifacts (usually a shoebox
or bucket full: apparently, these are the standard volumetric measures
for private artifact collections). Obviously, they have an archaeological
site, or perhaps many sites, on their property. But are those sites, in fact,
mounds? That is, are they intentionally constructed piles of earth created by prehistoric Indians?

Short answer: probably not. Mounds were constructed for at least
two reasons that we know of. Around two thousand years ago, rounded
conical mounds were built by Middle Woodland–period people as burial facilities, places where certain individuals were interred. We do not
know who those individuals were, or why they were buried in such special places. We are pretty sure that not everybody was buried in
mounds, however, as there just weren't that many mounds around. You
might think that to be buried in a special place, you had to be a special
person, someone with power, authority, rank, or prestige. Perhaps: but
if this is the case with Middle Woodland, it is not always evident in the
burials themselves. Sometimes burials are found with elaborate artifacts

made from exotic, imported raw materials. Archaeologists call such items "prestige goods." The copper ear spools mentioned in chapter 5 would be a good example. Other kinds of exotic goods found in Middle Woodland mounds include quartz crystals, cubes of galena (lead ore), elaborately decorated vessels, and artifacts that we call "boat stones" for want of a better word. These are smoothly ground pieces of rock, elongate and hollow inside, which do in fact look sort of like boats, although they are usually no longer than your hand. The inclusion of such out-of-the-ordinary artifacts, often made of imported raw materials, with burials would seem to indicate high status for the individuals interred. On the other hand, many burials in Middle Woodland mounds have absolutely nothing with them. Or at least nothing that has survived for us to see. So there are not clear indications of social rank, or class, unless burial in a mound was itself a way of denoting prestige. Perhaps the people buried in mounds were members of certain kin groups, or perhaps they were leaders of societies where prestige didn't accrue from the accumulation of stuff, but rather from sharing.

Archaeologists are fairly limited in trying to understand the social, political, and religious aspects of past cultures. We must beware the danger of trying to make everything we see in the past fit into what we have observed just in the last couple hundred years, as different "primitive" cultures around the world have been studied. The lure of the ethnographic record is quite strong, but trying to explain everything that happened in the past by reference to the ethnographic present is a dangerous practice indeed, as discussed in the last chapter. To use a different metaphor, it is like trying to explain the origins and evolution of metallurgy by studying a selection of guitar strings, or silverware, or doorknobs. It just isn't that easy. And a good thing, too, because if it were that easy, there'd be no reason to do archaeology!

But back to mounds. The other purpose that we know they were built to serve was as elevated platforms upon which buildings were

MISSISSIPPI FOCUS THE NATCHEZ

The people encountered by the French explorer La Salle in 1682 were the Natchez, a nation subsequently visited and described by many French and English traders and priests, and especially by the French who established a trading post and later a fort among the Natchez in the early 1700s. The ruler of the Natchez was known as the Great Sun, and he was revered by his people as a living, divine conduit between the physical and spiritual realms. His august personage was carried about on a litter. His brother, the Tattooed Serpent, was himself an important religious figure, as well as being the Natchez war chief. Upon Tattooed Serpent's death, which happened while the French were there, his wife and members of his entourage were sacrificed so that they could accompany the great man's spirit into the next world. The Grand Village of the Natchez was a ceremonial center where mounds were built, upon which stood the Great Sun's house and a temple where a sacred fire was kept burning. Visitors to the city of Natchez can visit this important site today.

The Great Sun of the Natchez being born on a litter. From an early 1700s drawing by Le Page Du Pratz, a Frenchman who ran a plantation in the Natchez Colony. Courtesy of the Mississippi Department of Archives and History.

erected. These wood and thatch buildings were either temples or houses for the religious and secular leaders of the day. At least, that's what their purpose was when Europeans actually saw them in use. And this astonishing historical incident took place in Mississippi, where the French encountered the last vestiges of what the Spaniard Hernando de Soto had seen a hundred and forty years earlier: the Mississippian cultures, who built platform mounds beginning about A.D. 1000.

So far, the picture is simple enough: conical burial mounds built during the Middle Woodland period about two thousand to fourteen hundred years ago, flat-topped platform mounds built during the Mississippi period about one thousand to five hundred years ago, with a few remnants of the latter left during the time of French exploration. That's pretty much what was still being taught to archaeology students not so very long ago. As is usually the case with archaeology, however, it turns out that things aren't that simple. In the mid-1980s, archaeologists began to suspect that something different was going on at some peculiar sites in the Southeast. Work by Dr. Robert Mainfort at the Pinson Mounds site in Tennessee, and by Dr. Janet Rafferty at the Ingomar Mounds site in Union County, Mississippi (see chapter 3), showed conclusively that at least some flat-topped mounds were, in fact, built during the Middle Woodland period, by the same people building the conical burial mounds. Since that time, several more sites in Mississippi have been shown to have Middle Woodland flat-topped mounds, including the famous Nanih Waiya site in Winston County, the Batesville Mounds near Batesville, and the Slate Springs mound site in Calhoun County.

What is at once exasperating and exciting is that, at present, archaeologists don't have a clue as to what these circa two-thousand-year-old flat-topped mounds were used for. They weren't used as burial mounds, nor did they have structures on them, or at least not structures that were substantial enough for archaeologists to find any traces of, something we're pretty good at in most cases. Obviously these impressive mounds—Ozier Mound at Pinson is thirty-three feet tall—were important to the people who built them. To call them "ceremonial" is probably accurate but frustratingly vague. Dr. Jay Johnson, of the University of Mississippi, has suggested that ritual feasting took place on the mound at Batesville, an intriguing suggestion. Unfortunately, concrete evidence for the function of Middle Woodland flat-topped mounds is proving hard to come by. Perhaps the development of more refined geophysical techniques like magnetometry (see chapter 3) will help to address this mystery.

A common misconception about many prehistoric mounds in Mississippi is that they are not "real." That is, they are not Indian mounds at all but were built by the state or federal government to *look like* Indian mounds! I have heard this same odd story about some of the finest mounds in the state, including the circa two-thousand-year-old Brogan burial mound just south of West Point on Highway 45, the huge Mound 14 at the Ingomar site in Union County, and, most frequently, the Mississippi-period Owl Creek Mounds in Chickasaw County. In some cases, it's easy to understand how such stories arose. The government has, in fact, rebuilt some mounds, such as those that had been excavated at the Middle Woodland–period Pharr site on the Natchez Trace (not all of the mounds at Pharr were excavated, by the way—or rebuilt as a consequence). But neither the state nor the federal government really had the time, money, or reason to go around building "Indian mounds" all over the place. I had the privilege of working at the Owl Creek Mounds in the summers of 1991 and 1992, when archaeologists from Mississippi State University were hired to obtain information about the site for interpretive purposes. The U.S. Forest Service owns two of the five mounds there. The other three are in private ownership, but the landowners kindly gave us permission to work on their land as well. While we were working, several local citizens came out and informed us—some gravely, some pityingly, some amusedly—that we were wasting our time because the mounds had been built with bulldozers back in the 1930s or 1940s.

How did such a story come about? Like much folklore, it contains an element of truth. The mounds *were* bulldozed, or at least some of them were. But they were not built by people on bulldozers; rather, the two mounds on government property were cleared of trees and "shaped up" decades ago. Certainly not the best management technique, but it's easy to see how local people subsequently came to believe that the mounds weren't real.

How do we know with certainty that any given mound is real? That is a very good question, as it happens—even archaeologists can be fooled by appearances. There are many natural high spots on the landscape that look a lot like conical burial mounds, for example. In the case of Owl Creek, we had old pictures from the Forest Service that showed people on bulldozers at the site. So how could we tell that the mounds were, in fact, real, and not something that had been constructed in the twentieth century?

I will answer these questions specifically for Owl Creek, but most of the kinds of evidence employed would pertain in any situation. At Owl Creek, the first thing we did was to turn to the historical records. Our first record of the site comes from the year 1805, when a doctor by the name of Rush Nutt visited and described the "ancient fortifications" in great detail. He mentioned five flat-topped mounds, located right where the five mounds are today. In 1935, a state archaeologist named Moreau Chambers worked at the site. The mounds were certainly there then, as Chambers dug trenches into four of them (he camped out on the biggest mound but didn't dig in it). He left a sketch map, a sheaf of notes, and many photographs of his work. Many years later, an archaeologist named Sam Brookes edited and published Chambers's notes. Chambers did not find what he was looking for (burials with artifacts

Owl Creek Mound 1, Chickasaw County, in 1935. Photo courtesy of Janet Rafferty.

Owl Creek Mound 1, Chickasaw County, in 1992.

Mississippi State University students working at the Owl Creek Mounds site, Chickasaw County. Photo courtesy of Janet Rafferty.

that could go in the state museum), but he did find many features left behind by the prehistoric Native Americans who built the mounds: *post holes*, wall trenches, and *fire hearths*.

In 1991 and 1992, Dr. Janet Rafferty led a team of students from Mississippi State University in excavations at the site. All five mounds were tested and the entire site was shovel tested on a twenty-meter grid. Overall artifact density was low, indicating that the site never had a large resident population. It also was low because the site was not used for very long. Several radiocarbon dates show that the mounds were built and used for perhaps only a century or so, around A.D. 1200. The artifacts that were found included pottery, stone arrow points, flakes, and a few small pieces of burned animal bone. More important were the features, which were found in abundance. Four of the mounds produced evidence of the structures that had stood upon them almost a thousand years ago. Wall trenches were quite common, for example, as were post

A small "smudge pit" full of charred corncobs found in Mound 1 at Owl Creek. Radiocarbon dating showed that the site was built and used over a short period about eight hundred years ago. Photo courtesy of Janet Rafferty.

holes—dark, circular stains marking where individually set posts once stood. The largest mound had several superimposed house floors, thin layers of brightly colored clays and sands that had been spread inside and outside the building on top of the mound. Dr. Rafferty also found there a kind of feature that archaeologists call a *smudge pit*, a small pit absolutely chock full of burned corncobs. The cobs are much smaller than ones you would see today, being the small-eared "Indian corn" grown by Native Americans in prehistoric times. What was such a feature for? Experiments have shown that if you fill a hole with cobs and set them on fire, you get a lot of smoke. Archaeologists assume that this is the effect that the builders of the mounds were after. Why make smoke? Because it's useful for keeping insects away, perhaps. But this particular smudge pit's location, on top of a mound, makes one wonder if the smoke was for "special effect" purposes.

Dr. Rafferty also found plenty of evidence relating to the (much) later bulldozer work at the mounds. One mound, for example, had about four feet of dirt pushed up on top of it. The dirt was full of nails, glass, and other artifacts from some old house site that had been bulldozed up from nearby. It also was clear that a big chunk had been taken out of the north side of the mound at some time in the past, probably for use as road fill. Beneath all that disturbance, however, she found what was left of the mound itself. How can we be sure? Because of the way mounds were built, one basketload of dirt at a time. Such *basketloading* produces a very characteristic archaeological signature, as each individual load of dirt is slightly different in color and texture. The result in an excavation unit is a beautiful *profile* (the unit wall) with one lens-shaped blob of dirt on top of another, on top of another, on top of another, and so on. Once you've seen basketloading, you'll never fail to recognize it again, especially if you're an archaeologist who is trained to "read" soils. We can look at a profile and tell how deep earthworms have penetrated in the ground, for example. So telling the difference between ancient basketloads of dirt, which contained prehistoric pottery and other artifacts, and the massively disturbed, bulldozed layer on top really wasn't much of a challenge. The local passersby weren't giving us much credit to think that we couldn't figure out what was "real" and what wasn't at the site.

If you're still not convinced (folktales die hard!), let me tell you what else Dr. Rafferty found in the disturbed mound. Her goal was to learn as much as she could while doing as little damage as possible to what was left of the mound itself (obviously, it had already suffered enough damage). Thanks to Chambers, she had an opportunity to do just that. In his notes and maps, he described a long trench he had excavated on an east-west line almost completely through the mound. With her trained eye, Dr. Rafferty was able to spot the subtle outlines of Chambers's trench when the bulldozed layer had been removed from

Above: Basketloading seen in the profile of an excavation unit in a mound at the Middle Woodland–period Ingomar site in Union County. Each dark, lens-shaped blob represents one individual basketload of dirt that was dumped by Indians when the mound was being constructed. Photo courtesy of Janet Rafferty.

Left: Basketloading seen in the profile of an excavation unit in the Mississippi-period mound at the Lyon's Bluff site in Oktibbeha County.

the top of the mound. She was then able to clean the trench out, and to study the profiles in a more modern fashion. At the very bottom of the trench, she found two glass bottles that Chambers had left there. And like something out of a movie, one of the bottles had a note in it! Chambers had written the note almost sixty years earlier, placed it in the bottle, sealed it up with wax, and buried it in the mound when he backfilled his trench. The note gave his name and the names of his crewmembers, as well as stating: "This mound excavated in the month of August, 1935." The results of Dr. Rafferty's work can be seen on the excellent interpretive signs erected by the U.S. Forest Service at the site.

A bottle containing a note left inside Mound 2 at the Owl Creek site by Moreau Chambers in 1935. Photo courtesy of Janet Rafferty.

(Some years later I went back to do a little more work at Owl Creek, on a part of the site east of the mounds that hadn't been closely examined before. I happened to have with me three young women from England who were on a summer internship with the Forest Service. On one particularly fine, summer morning, a local farmer on a horse-drawn wagon came down the road that runs through the site. The interns were delighted; they grabbed their cameras and dashed over to capture a bit of Mississippiana to show their friends back home. I remained in the excavation unit we were digging. As I worked, I heard a gravelly voice ask, in a classic southern drawl, "You married, lil' darlin'?" When the rather startled interns returned, I felt obliged to explain to them that Mississippi is known as "the Hospitality State.")

The prehistoric native inhabitants of Mississippi built other kinds of earthworks besides mounds. Especially during the Middle Woodland period, large linear or curvilinear embankments were raised. These sometimes take the form of semicircles, with the open side abutting a river or creek. These earthworks could attain an impressive size, being hundreds of yards across. Several years ago, Sam Brookes received a call from a man who needed an archaeological survey done in Sharkey County where he wanted to put a culvert on his land. The Mississippi Department of Archives and History required the survey because a very large and famous site called Little Spanish Fort—a semicircular, Middle Woodland earthwork—was in the vicinity. Some years previously another archaeologist had stated that the site had been destroyed by agriculture, and the department wanted to see if anything was left. When Sam arrived at the spot, he noticed what appeared to be an old tramline—a railroad embankment—nearby. A little further on, he was astonished to see a large mound rising up out of an agricultural field. Large mounds don't occur naturally in the Delta, so he knew immediately that he was looking at an Indian mound. Upon further investigation, he found that the "tramline," a raised bank of earth about three feet high, ran for some distance through the woods and curved out into the field. Sam realized that he was looking at Little Spanish Fort—it was not destroyed after all! Fortuitous circumstance led, in this case, to a happy ending: the landowner got his culvert put in (it turned out to be at a point off the site), the record got straightened out, and a very, very important site was rediscovered.

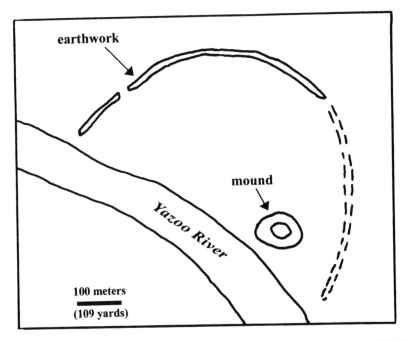

A plan view of the Little Spanish Fort site in Sharkey County. This large, Middle Woodland–period earthwork is one of a series of similar sites found in the lower Yazoo Basin of west-central Mississippi. The earthwork is a raised embankment that today stands about six feet high in places; it probably was higher in the past. The dotted lines show where the earthwork has been plowed down. Adapted from Figure 2 in H. Edwin Jackson, "Little Spanish Fort: An Early Middle Woodland Enclosure in the Lower Yazoo Basin, Mississippi," *Midcontinental Journal of Archaeology* 23, no. 2 (1998): 199–220.

Little Spanish Fort has nothing to do with Spaniards, as it happens. Nor is it a fort. Many earthworks were called "forts" early on, before archaeologists demonstrated that they were prehistoric features. They do look sort of like defensive earthworks, but probably didn't serve that function as the embankments aren't really high enough to be defensive walls, and as it would take thousands of people to defend such large areas. How large? Dr. Ed Jackson, of the University of Southern Mississippi, led a team of students in mapping and excavating at Little Spanish Fort after its rediscovery. Detailed mapping showed that the earthwork, charcoal from which was radiocarbon-dated to about 100 B.C., enclosed approximately forty-five acres of land! Another reason to believe that the earthwork was not a defensive feature is that there apparently wasn't much inside it to defend. There was no large village, but only the remains of a small habitation area adjacent to the Yazoo River. Interestingly, the mound enclosed by the earthwork may be of somewhat later construction than the embankment itself, based on the types of pottery recovered. Little Spanish Fort is one of three such large, semicircular embankment sites located along the Sunflower and Yazoo rivers in the lower Yazoo Basin of Mississippi. The Jackson's Landing site in Hancock County is yet another site with a semicircular, Middle Woodland–period earthwork. As of yet we really don't know what these earthworks signify. These are certainly world-class sites, however, and we are fortunate that they are part of the archaeological heritage of Mississippi.

We have solved many mysteries where mounds are concerned, but even as we learn more about them, other mysteries arise. For example, we now know that conical mounds, once thought to have been a diagnostic feature of the Middle Woodland period, were also built during the Middle Archaic period, some three thousand years earlier. Dr. Joe Saunders has reported on such Middle Archaic mounds in northeastern Louisiana. The Watson Brake site in Ouachita Parish, for example, has eleven mounds joined by a low earthwork to form a rough circle almost three hundred yards across. These Middle Archaic mounds do not seem to contain burials: artifacts that have been found inside them include a kind of funny, double-notched spear point called an Evans Point and, curiously, small clay cubes without any markings or decoration. This was before pottery was being made in North America, so no pots or other clay artifacts besides the puzzling cubes have been found. As of yet, we do not know with certainty whether any of these Middle Archaic mounds exist in Mississippi, but I wouldn't be surprised if we have several. In fact, a likely candidate was recently identified in Lincoln County by archaeologists working for the Mississippi Department of Transportation. And to think that, when I was a boy, people told me there was no use trying to become an archaeologist because "they've figured all that stuff out already"! We have only just begun to wrap our heads around the richness and complexity that is the archaeological record of Mississippi. There is enough archaeology out there for ten thousand archaeologists and enough mysteries to keep us all busy for a long, long time to come.

WHAT WERE THE ARTIFACTS USED FOR, AND HOW WERE THEY MADE?

Remember the arrowhead that I described in chapter 1, the one that I found in Choctaw County as a boy? People often refer to such artifacts as "bird points," the idea being that anything so small must have been fashioned for a particular purpose. What is small enough to hunt with such a small point? Birds are, or so many people like to think, and hence the name. The larger points commonly found are more generally referred to as "arrowheads." This is one of the most common errors that I hear when I talk to people across the state about archaeology. There are many other misconceptions as well, and in this chapter I would like to lay some of the more common myths to rest.

Let's start with the points. What people don't realize is that most of the stone points found in Mississippi aren't "arrowheads" at all; they are spear points. These take many forms. Some have stems that were set down into a piece of stout cane or a wooden shaft. When they broke, they commonly snapped off at the stem, and if you are a collector, you probably have picked up some of the stems themselves (flaked stone objects that are flat on both ends, shaped like compressed ovals). Some

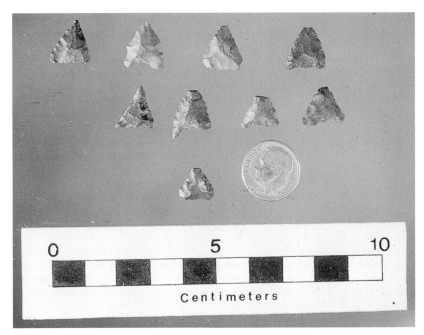

Small, stone arrow points, usually called "triangular points" by archaeologists.

spear points have notches so that they could be bound in a split-wood shaft. One thing that they all have in common is that they are pretty large and fairly heavy, not good attributes for arrow points. Spears were used by the first inhabitants of what is now Mississippi and continued to be used for thousands and thousands of years, with the forms of the points gradually changing over time. Those changes in form are one thing that archaeologists use to tell how old a particular kind of point is, using relative dating (see chapter 4).

The bow and arrow showed up in Mississippi somewhere around the year A.D. 600, at about the beginning of the Late Woodland period, and the new weaponry caught on fairly rapidly. Prehistoric *flintknappers* (people who work stone) made some arrow points with small stems and/or notches, like miniature spear points, while some were simple, *triangular points.* These are the only stone "arrowheads" there are. These were not used solely for hunting birds. In fact, it's fairly doubtful if they were *ever* used to hunt birds. Think about it—if you're a bow hunter, do you waste your time shooting arrows into the air, or up into trees? To kill roosting turkeys, perhaps, but otherwise arrows were used to hunt deer and other animals.

The bow and arrow also had an effect on prehistoric warfare. The first human burials that I excavated were eroding out of the riverbank on the Tennessee-Tombigbee waterway. A local collector had seen what he thought were two cannonballs sticking out of the riverbank. Upon closer inspection, the "cannonballs" turned out to be skulls. They were Late Woodland–period burials, about twelve hundred years old. I was part of the crew that salvaged that portion of the site before the bank could erode so far that burials started falling into the river, and before the gravesite came to the attention of pothunters. I will never forget the day when a friend of mine, working with me on the burial, struck something with his metal dental pick that went "tink." Bone does not go "tink." He carefully exposed the bottom of the rib that he was working on, and we both were astonished to see a stone arrow point imbedded for half its length in the bone. By the time that we were done excavating the burial, we had found four arrow points in the skeleton, and who knows how many arrows had been stuck in the flesh when the individual was slain? The burial was that of a young man, who was respectably large for the time at about five and a half feet tall. He had been hit from behind, perhaps in an ambush as he went down to the river over a thousand years ago. Evidence for this type of hit-and-run warfare is common in the Late Woodland period along the Tombigbee River, with men, women, and children having been thus killed. As noted in chapter 6, we are only just beginning to understand that turbulent time in the prehistory of Mississippi.

Another very common myth concerns how Indians made flaked-stone tools. The idea is that they first heated rocks up and then caused them to flake by dripping cold water on them. I can hazard two guesses as to how this particular misconception came into being. The first is that lots of flakes are found near streams. This is simply a result of people living next to good water: no real mystery there. The second possibility is that people have noticed that fire does funny things to rock, like change its color, for example. Many, many projectile points, other stone tools, and flakes found in Mississippi are a striking red color. Most of them didn't start out that way: when obtained from a river bar as fresh gravel by a prehistoric flintknapper, they were brown or yellow, no different from the gravel in a gravel road today. Heating the stone makes it easier to flake and also turns it red. If you see red pebbles in asphalt, this is what happened to them before the asphalt cooled. So yes, Native Americans did heat-treat their rocks, but they did not flake them by dripping cold water on them while they were hot. I know from personal experience what happens if you try this, as I nearly put my eye out with an exploding piece of gravel during one enthusiastic but ill-considered experiment as a youth. The rocks simply shatter, producing nothing of use. It is far more likely that rocks were buried in shallow pits, with fires then being built over the pits after a thin layer of dirt was put down to produce heat that gradually brought about the desired changes in workability.

Points and other flaked stone artifacts were actually made with tools of stone and bone. A hard *hammerstone* was first used to remove flakes from a piece of gravel or other rock. Next, softer hammers of bone or wood were used to further reduce the piece. This process of reducing a piece of rock by striking it with some sort of hammer is called *percussion flaking*. Deer antler works especially well for soft-hammer percussion. Once the point is near completion, it is finished by *pressure flaking*, that is, by pushing small flakes off the edges using the tip of a deer antler tine or some other small tool. With practice, this process is easier than it sounds. An experienced flintknapper can whip out a perfectly respectable spear point or arrowhead in less than twenty minutes.

THE ART OF FLINTKNAPPING

Archaeologists have learned a lot about the mechanics of stone-tool manufacture in the last few decades, largely by trying to make stone tools themselves. Three stages of manufacture—hard-hammer percussion, soft-hammer percussion, and pressure flaking—are sufficient to produce most of the kinds of flaked stone tools found at sites. Each step yields a product that also is recognizable in itself. Hard-hammer percussion with a hammerstone produces an early stage *preform*, which is then shaped with a soft-hammer baton to form a late-stage preform. If you've ever found what looks like a spear point or arrowhead that isn't quite finished, that's probably what you've got. Pressure flaking completes the shaping of the point and creates sharp, durable edges. Many different kinds of rock break in the way necessary for them to be used for flaked stone tools. Ordinary gravel works fine, with practice. If you want to try flintknapping yourself, you can find suppliers of tools and good rock on the Internet, or you can try finding the materials yourself. If you flintknap outdoors, please do it on a blanket, a tarp, or something else so that you can collect all the flakes and dispose of them in the garbage. This is very important, because the flakes you produce will be indistinguishable from the real thing, and if you do not collect them you will be creating a "site" that might confuse archaeologists for all time. I, for one, am confused enough already, so please remember this suggestion if you try your hand at the ancient art of making stone tools.

"Tommyhawks" is another one that I hear about a lot. If you think that you have one of these in the shoebox in the closet, you are not quite correct. True tomahawks are small, metal axes that were traded in great quantity to northeastern Indian tribes such as the Iroquois. If you've ever found something made of stone that looks sort of like an axe, then what you probably have is, indeed, an axe. The prehistoric Indians of Mississippi did plenty of clearing of the land; as you will remember from chapter 6, they became farmers about a thousand years ago, and I have yet to meet the farmer who can grow corn in the shade. They cut down trees for all kinds of other reasons as well: for canoes, for house materials, for palisades, for fuel, and probably for things we don't even know about today. To cut down trees, you need an axe, and before the Europeans came over there were no metal axes to be had. So the Indians made axe heads of stone, hafted them into wooden handles, and found them to be perfectly adequate for the everyday business of felling trees.

There is a particular kind of stone axe that most often has the "tommyhawk" label mistakenly attached. This is a smooth, polished axe called a *celt* by archaeologists (pronounced "selt"). These beautiful artifacts are often made of stone that was imported from long distances away, especially a kind of metamorphic rock called *greenstone*; and indeed, many celts are greenish in color. These also were used as axes are used, being hafted into heavy wooden handles. No doubt they made effective war clubs as well. We know pretty well what the handles looked like, because of an astonishing find made in Alabama, where a man checking his trotline in the Black Warrior River brought up a celt, still in its

A stone axe from Pontotoc County. Probably Middle Archaic period. Photo courtesy of Janet Rafferty.

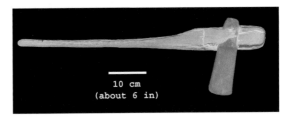

A greenstone celt still in its wooden handle, found in the Black Warrior River in Alabama. Photo courtesy of the University of Alabama Museums.

wooden handle! This lucky gentleman then did something very admirable; instead of taking the thing home and putting it up above his mantle where the handle would soon have disintegrated, he took it to the museum at the Moundville Archaeological Park. There, the whole thing was treated with preservatives (see chapter 11), and a rare and very important find was saved for all time.

WHAT ARE THEY; HOW WERE THEY MADE?

Sandstone pitted stones from Attala County. The white marks are where archaeologists wrote provenience information on the artifacts. Photo courtesy of the Mississippi Department of Archives and History.

Some of the myths that emerge concerning artifacts are downright weird. The famous Clovis points, for example, are "fluted," meaning that long, thin flakes were struck from the bottom of the point up one or both sides, producing shallow channels running up the center of the point (see figure on page 52). This presumably was related to the way that the large spear points were hafted into wooden shafts. According to folklore, however, there is a more grisly explanation. The flutes are "blood channels," designed to speed the demise of the stricken prey by providing a way for blood to flow out more freely!

While some common stories about what artifacts were used for are clearly not believable, there are others that should not be written off lightly. For example, if you are an artifact collector in Mississippi, you have doubtless found what many people call "nutting stones," fairly small pieces of sandstone or other rock with one or more pits worked into the middle. Were these *pitted stones* used as anvils for cracking nuts, as many people believe? Probably so. They also likely served as anvils for other tasks as well, such as breaking other rocks to produce flakes of a particular shape useful for small tools, a process called *bipolar flaking*. One story you will commonly hear about pitted stones is not true, however. Because the rocks are generally pretty small, rather flat, and have a pit on both sides, your thumb and middle finger will quite comfortably fit into the opposing pits. Many people have tried to convince me that the pits were made for just that purpose—to provide a way to grasp the rock so that it could be used as a hammer. There are two reasons why I don't believe this. The first is that we know what real hammerstones look like: they are tough cobbles of quartzite, easily recognized by the battered ends produced by repeated use. I use one myself when I flint-knap, and if I dropped my hammerstone on an archaeological site, no professional would be able to tell that it wasn't prehistoric. The second reason that I don't believe pitted stones were used as hammers is a simple matter of physics. If you grasp a pitted stone between your thumb and middle finger and try to strike a blow with it, you can deliver about as much force as a malnourished leprechaun with a wiffle bat. Hardly an effective hammer, and hardly worth the trouble of working finger-tip-sized pits into the face of a rock that you can easily hold in your hand already.

My favorite story concerning the misidentification of an artifact comes from a friend who worked as an archaeologist with the Mississippi Department of Archives and History in Jackson. People frequently bring artifacts in to the department to have them identified. Often, they bring along their own homespun interpretations as well. In this particular case, a man came in with a large, sandstone *grinding stone*. These common artifacts were used to grind plant foods into meal or flour, resulting over time in a sort of scooped-out slab. The fellow bringing it in, however, had developed his own novel hypothesis concerning the function of this particular artifact. It was, he gravely informed the

A sandstone grinding stone from north Mississippi. These artifacts were used with smaller stones to crush and grind seeds.

flabbergasted archaeologists, a "deer-whackin' rock." He then explained in elaborate detail how it worked. An enterprising Native American hunter would scale a tree overhanging a game trail. Heavy sandstone slab in his lap, he would wait patiently until an unsuspecting deer made its way down the trail and passed beneath the tree. At just the crucial moment, the hunter would drop from the tree, land on the back of the startled deer, lock his feet under the animal's belly, and proceed to "whack him on the head" with the deer-whackin' rock! As support for this innovative explanation, the gentleman pointed out how repeated deer-whackin' episodes had gradually worn the rock down in the middle. Although I have serious doubts about the efficiency of this proposed hunting technique, I certainly can't fault him for his imagination.

One final misconception I would like to lay to rest concerns the discipline itself. Archaeologists don't study dinosaurs! This particular idea is so prevalent that the students in my Intro to Archaeology class often get it wrong on their first exam. Fossils—of dinosaurs or otherwise—are interesting, no doubt about it. I find them as fascinating as the next person. But a professional paleontologist would blush to learn how little I really know about them. Fossils are the remains of once-living creatures, turned to rock, or some trace in rock. Archaeologists also study traces, but the traces left behind by one particular kind of life—people! And to do that we study artifacts. So when people bring fossils to me, asking for information, I send them across the street to where the geologists hang out. But if you're in town, feel free to visit me as well. Especially if you have some artifacts you'd like for me to see.

WHAT ARE MY ARTIFACTS WORTH?

Of all the questions that I am frequently asked, this is the only one that I hate. Especially when a young boy or girl is doing the asking. What are archaeological remains worth? Why, they are priceless, of course, because they provide a window into an almost unknown world. Their scientific value is inestimable. But what are they worth in monetary terms? To be honest, I don't know. Archaeologists aren't in the business of marketing artifacts, nor should you be.

And here's why. Once a monetary value is placed on artifacts, they begin to be bought and sold. The problem with this is supply and demand. There is, unfortunately, a market for artifacts, especially now that things can be bought and sold over the Internet. Artifacts from Mississippi are being sold this way even as you read. Please do not participate in this sordid business. Not only is the acquisition and sale of artifacts morally wrong because it leads to important, irreplaceable sites being destroyed, but there also may very well be legal issues involved. Without knowing it, if you purchase an artifact over the Internet or at a flea market, or anywhere else for that matter, you may become an accessory to a felony.

Why? Because, as discussed in chapter 5, Native Americans didn't throw away whole pots or beautiful stone artifacts any more than we would throw away beautiful and useful artifacts today. The reason that such elaborate and impressive artifacts exist in the archaeological record is because they were buried with people. When you see whole pots for sale at a flea market, someone has *dug them up out of a human grave*. This is against the law, even if the site is on private land. It is the same law that says it's not OK to go and dig up the local graveyard. And if artifacts were obtained illegally—say, by picking them up off the ground while trespassing on someone's farm—then you also can be held responsible if you buy them, whether you knew that they were illegally obtained or not. Did you know that, according to the Mississippi Antiquities Law, you are supposed to have written permission to collect artifacts on someone's land? The law reads as follows:

> No person, not being owner thereof, and without the written consent of the owner, proprietor, lessee, or person in charge thereof, shall enter or attempt to enter upon the lands of another and intentionally injure, disfigure, remove, excavate, damage, take, dig into, or destroy any historical structure, monument, marker, medallion, or artifact, or any prehistoric or historic archaeological site, American Indian or aboriginal remains located in, on or under any private lands within the State of Mississippi. No person without a permit [from the Mississippi Department of Archives and History's Board of Trustees] . . . and without written permission of the landowner, shall intentionally injure, disfigure, remove, excavate, damage, take, dig into, or destroy any prehistoric or historic American Indian or aboriginal burial.

So if someone tries to sell you something, either in person or over the Internet, ask him to show you the signed letter of permission. Odds are he won't have such a thing, which means that you are dealing with a criminal, and very possibly with someone who has had his hands in a grave.

Let's say that someone goes out onto someone else's land and picks up some spear points. While he's there, he spots a midden and probes it with the metal rod he carries for just such occasions. With a practiced hand, he can tell when the rod encounters a prehistoric pot. He digs and finds the pot . . . sitting beside the skull of the person it was buried with centuries ago. He takes his prize and hurries away before the landowner catches him. Now your cousin comes visiting from Alabama, or Tennessee, or some other state, and spots the pot for sale on the Internet, at a flea market, or at some country store. He buys it, not knowing where it came from, and takes it back home. Your cousin is now open to a visit from the FBI, for he has just transported illegally gotten goods across a state line. He has just committed a misdemeanor under state law, and a felony under federal law, prosecutable under the *Archaeological Resources Protection Act* of 1976. Whatever that pot might be worth to him, it isn't worth that kind of trouble.

Let me be clear at this point about the difference between pothunters and collectors. The former are criminals. The latter include some of the finest people that it has ever been my pleasure to know. Collecting, if done right, can be not only fun but also a very useful enterprise. I have spent many productive hours talking to collectors, looking at their artifacts, answering their questions, and having some of my own questions answered in turn. Several times I have had concerned collectors alert me to situations where sites that they knew about were being destroyed. On more than one occasion, their quick actions in that regard have led to some very important sites being saved or salvaged. Conscientious collectors are willing to learn and are equally willing to share what they know, which can be a lot. This is a priceless contribution, because there aren't that many archaeologists in the world and we simply can't be everywhere at once. Many good and caring people therefore serve as the eyes and ears of the archaeological community. Some have even taken their interest so far that they have written articles about their findings,

MISSISSIPPI FOCUS

BIOGRAPHY OF AN AVOCATIONAL ARCHAEOLOGIST

Carey Geiger is an avocational archaeologist who has been very active in Mississippi. Ted Brown, a member of the Mississippi Archaeological Association, introduced Geiger to artifact collecting and study. They have teamed together since 1970. One of the sites they located was the Beaumont Gravel Pit site in Perry County, which contained material from all but the earliest part of Mississippi's prehistory. Their findings prompted professional archaeologists to become involved with their research. Sam McGahey, Sam Brookes, and John Connaway from the Mississippi Department of Archives and History (MDAH) excavated at Beaumont in the early 1970s. Geiger and Brown continued to excavate under MDAH's supervision. Brookes and McGahey assisted them in lab analysis and report writing. Dr. Al Goodyear and James Michie of the University of South Carolina also assisted. Goodyear visited the site, studied the artifacts, and provided guidance on the research. Dr. Clarence Webb, a renowned avocational archaeologist with a national reputation, also visited the site and provided counsel. Archaeologists in Arkansas, Texas, Arizona, Alabama, and Florida cooperated with Geiger and Brown on their research. Dr. Ervin Otvos, a geologist with the Gulf Coast Research Laboratory,

Carey Geiger, an avocational archaeologist and long-time member of the Mississippi Archaeological Association.

provided them with geological information related to the site. Two preliminary reports were written and published in the journal *Mississippi Archaeology* (Geiger, vol. 15, 1980; Geiger and Brown, vol. 18, 1983).

When Geiger moved from the state, all of the excavated artifacts, field notes, and other documents were archived at the University of Southern Mississippi's anthropology department with the help of Dr. Ed Jackson. Joseph Giliberti, then a graduate student at USM, wrote his master's thesis on the Beaumont excavation.

Geiger returned to Mississippi, where he has served as president of the Mississippi Archaeological Association and as statewide coordinator for Mississippi Archaeology Month. He is continuing his research and is writing a graphical and statistical analysis report on the Beaumont excavation. His work has been recognized in two books, *The Paleoindian and Early Archaic Southeast* (David G. Anderson and Kenneth E. Sassaman; Tuscaloosa: University of Alabama Press, 1996) and *Selected Preforms, Points, and Knives of the North American Indians, Volume 2* (Gregory Perino; Idabel, Oklahoma: Points and Barbs Press, 1991). Geiger has recently been assisting Dr. Goodyear at a very early site in South Carolina. He plans to continue working in archaeology as long as possible. Geiger states, "Any amateur who hunts and collects arrowheads without cooperating with professional archaeologists is missing out on the greatest experience. It is thrilling when you realize that you can contribute to the archaeological understanding of Mississippi and the southeastern United States."

making their own intellectual contributions to the world. I have enormous respect for collectors who care enough about the things that they find to learn how to do things the right way, and I am proud to call many of them my friends.

Pothunters, on the other hand, view the archaeological community with disdain, just as they do the laws that should prevent them from looting and the landowners whose property they violate. I have talked with many people who were hovering between the two worlds of proper collecting (sometimes called *avocational archaeology*) and pothunting. As collectors, they were interested in artifacts and what could be learned from them; but they also had caught the scent of money and were trying to find justifications for crossing over to what I, being of the *Star Wars* generation, think of as "the Dark Side." I understand the temptation—like many people in Mississippi, I grew up poor—but I would like to believe that anyone with an honest heart and mind would, in time, see those justifications for the rationalizations that they really are. In the hope of aiding those who might be struggling with themselves over such matters, I would like to dissect three of the more common rationalizations for pothunting that I have heard.

Rationalization #1—"It's all been plowed through anyway, so why not dig it up?"

It is entirely true that the landscape of the Southeast has been extensively farmed, in some places for over two hundred years. Obviously, this has caused a lot of disturbance to the archaeological record. But one never knows what remains intact beneath the plow zone. Some sites are very deep, a result of the buildup of artifacts and midden over centuries or even millennia. I have been privileged to work at the Lyon's Bluff site, an extraordinary Mississippi-period mound and village complex in Oktibbeha County. The site was occupied by Native Americans over a period of some four hundred and fifty years, from about A.D. 1200 to 1650, during which time over six feet of midden laden with pottery,

A concentration of ca. two-thousand-year-old pottery sherds found just below the surface of a site in Oktibbeha County. Photo courtesy of Janet Rafferty.

animal bones, mussel shells, and other artifacts piled up. The site had been farmed for decades, but the plow penetrated to a depth of only about a foot, meaning that most of the archaeology there remains intact. Even sites that aren't that deep can still have many features preserved below the plow zone. I have seen hilltop sites in Oktibbeha County, for example, where human burials are preserved in pits dug by Native Americans into the stiff clay subsoil. The topsoil on the ridges has long since been loosened by farming and washed away. But the pits and their burials remain, as do other features, often only inches below the surface. As discussed in chapter 3, even sites that have been completely plowed through can still yield important information via a controlled surface collection. And, of course, if someone is digging up whole pots, or caches of spear points or other intact artifacts, then it's pretty clear that not everything has been destroyed by the plow, right?

Rationalization #2—"If I don't dig it up, someone else will."

This is a pretty poor excuse to go out and destroy something important, especially if it involves breaking the law, as grave robbing certainly does. Let's look at it from a purely ethical standpoint, by comparing what happens when someone loots archaeological sites to what happens when someone poaches an endangered animal species. In the green forest of East Africa, there lives one of the most striking animals on that continent, the magnificent black-and-white colobus monkey, *Colobus guereza*. These primates are unusual in a number of ways, including the fact that they are specialized leaf-eaters. To break down the tough leaves, they have multichambered stomachs, like cows! They will occasionally leave the trees to wade, waist deep, in small pools, gathering nutrient-rich aquatic plants. They are born pure white, and the color of their hair gradually changes to a rich, glossy black, except for startling, long, white shanks that fall from their shoulders and large, white tufts at the ends of their amazingly long tails. One subspecies also has a frame of purest white around the dark, red-eyed face, a combination that an artist would be hard-pressed to create.

Those beautiful pelts were almost the colobines' undoing. During the late nineteenth century, it became fashionable for women of means in Europe and North America to wear them as capes. Over the space of several years, an incredible two million monkeys were killed to meet the fickle vagaries of fashion. This human behavior, which pushed the colobines to the edge of extinction, was dishearteningly selfish and shortsighted. Was being "in style" really so important that it was worth killing all those remarkable animals? Of course not. Every woman who made the social scene wearing a colobine pelt draped around her shoulders was an accessory to a crime against nature. To defend her actions by saying that "everyone else was doing it" is no defense. A crime is a crime. And becoming a criminal—a *legally recognized* criminal—by looting burials cannot be defended on the grounds that other criminals are already out there.

There is, of course, one major difference between endangered species and archaeological sites. Endangered species, if managed properly, can come back. The colobus monkey is a good example. Although they were still the victims of poaching, wide-scale commercial hunting declined as the pelts fell out of fashion, and the colobines' numbers grew until they are now considered a "lower risk" species in terms of conservation (the chief threat to them now comes from habitat destruction). Unfortunately, such success cannot be replicated at archaeological sites. Once they are destroyed, they are destroyed for all time. No amount of management will bring them back. In the parlance of land managers, they are a *non-renewable resource*. Rationalizations for their destruction are accordingly that much harder to defend.

Rationalization #3—"Archaeologists dig that stuff up, so why can't I?"

Archaeologists are not after personal gain, nor are we after private collections. We do not sell the artifacts, nor do we hoard them for ourselves. We are paid to do a job, which is to save as much as possible in the face of ongoing destruction and to try and learn more about the stuff and the people who made it. We devote long years of our lives to obtain the training necessary to accomplish these tasks. The artifacts that we obtain are stored in special places so as to be available to others who are interested in them. Do archaeologists excavate pots? Of course we do, if circumstances warrant. Are archaeologists pothunters? No. We are highly skilled professionals in a highly technical field. And a looted site, to an archaeologist, is a horrible, horrible thing to behold.

As important as prehistoric sites are, they are only a part of Mississippi's cultural heritage. Civil War sites are another part that is seriously in jeopardy. Why? Because the same type of person who thinks that it's OK to loot Indian graves also thinks that it's just fine to sneak around in a national military park with a metal detector at night. Imagine grown men, dressed in camouflage, faces painted, caught in the spotlight with shovels in hand. This has happened more than once. In the late 1980s, an observant citizen notified officials that some people were digging in Vicksburg National Military Park. Thanks to that tip, two men with metal detectors, shovels, probe rods, and the other paraphernalia of looters were caught red-handed. A third member of the team ran, but was later caught. Not only were the three men heavily fined, but their truck and all of their equipment was confiscated and they were given probationary sentences. According to park historian Terry Winschel, several other people have been caught metal-detecting in the park since then, with varying punishments being levied against them. Recently, one man was prosecuted for ripping a piece of wood off the Union ironclad USS *Cairo* in broad daylight! Seems he wanted a souvenir for his naval history collection. The problem of site looting is a never-ending one, and it is growing every year.

What can be done about this ongoing, criminal destruction of Mississippi's archaeological remains? For starters, law enforcement officers and judges need to be familiar with the laws and to take the enforcement of those laws seriously. The main ones that every representative of the legal system in Mississippi should review are the Mississippi Antiquities Law, the Mississippi Cemetery Laws, and the Archaeological Resources Protection Act of 1979. There are many other pertinent laws as well.

Every citizen of Mississippi should be aware that it is against the law to dig up Indian (or any other) burials without a permit from the Mississippi Department of Archives and History, that written permission is needed to surface-hunt for artifacts on other people's land, and that digging for artifacts is inherently destructive. You don't have to be an expert on historic preservation laws to recognize when a site is being looted. You, too, can be the eyes and ears of Mississippi. If you come across a site that has been looted—usually pretty easy to recognize by the pits, mounds of dirt, discarded cigarette butts, and so on—what should you do? First of all, remember that you may be looking at a

WHAT DO THE LAWS SAY?

There are many historic preservation laws in the United States, and legislation continues to be produced or revised every year. A few of the more important laws and some of their main provisions are listed here.

The Antiquities Act of 1906 gives the president the power to designate as national monuments "historic landmarks, historic and prehistoric structures, and other objects of historic or scientific interest that are situated upon the land owned or controlled by the Government of the United States." Such designation provides extra protection for important sites on federal lands.

The Historic Sites Act of 1935 gives the secretary of the interior the power to acquire important historical properties by gift or through purchase, and to make cooperative agreements with individuals or entities to protect and enhance important sites.

The Reservoir Salvage Act of 1960 provides for "the preservation of historical and archaeological data which might otherwise be lost or destroyed as the result of flooding [and associated development of roads, etc.] caused by the construction of a dam" by the government or by a contractor using government funds.

The National Historic Preservation Act of 1966 is our most important historic preservation law. It formalized the National Register of Historic Places, required states to prepare comprehensive preservation plans, required federal agencies to "take into account" the effects of their actions on historic properties, and established the Advisory Council on Historic Preservation. Amendments to the law provided tax breaks for developers and individuals who rehabilitate historic properties and directed federal agencies to use existing historic structures where feasible.

The Archeological and Historic Preservation Act of 1974 allows federal agencies to spend up to one percent of budgeted project funds to have archaeological surveys and salvage work done.

The American Indian Religious Freedom Act of 1978 states that "it shall be the policy of the United States to protect and preserve for American Indians their inherent right to freedom to believe, express, and exercise [their] traditional religions." This includes having access to sacred sites and artifacts.

The Archaeological Resources Protection Act of 1979 established stiff penalties for persons looting or defacing archaeological properties on public lands. ARPA also can apply to private land if other laws (e.g., burial desecration or trespassing) are broken.

The Cultural Property Implementation Act of 1983 committed the United States to abide by the United Nations Educational, Scientific, and Cultural Organization convention controlling the illicit trafficking of antiquities across international borders. The looting of archaeological sites is a problem worldwide. So be careful what you buy abroad!

The Abandoned Shipwreck Act of 1987 protects shipwrecks in rivers and within three miles of the coast by asserting U.S. ownership and then turning title over to the states. Under this law, such wrecks are exempt from salvage laws; sport diving is allowed under regulation.

The Native American Graves Protection and Repatriation Act of 1990 required all federally funded agencies to inventory their archaeological holdings, to evaluate which human remains or artifacts could be affiliated with an existing tribe, and to provide that information to any tribe that requested it. Where affiliation can be demonstrated, the materials are turned over if the tribe so desires.

crime scene: leave the evidence alone! Second, contact the landowner and let him know that someone has been digging on his land. If the landowner is willing, the local police should be notified. If that happens, don't let them treat the situation in a light manner (remember, it's not "just Indian stuff"). Breaking the law is a serious business, especially if it involves grave robbing, and serious problems deserve the serious attention of our law enforcement officials.

I do know one professional in the state, a very dear friend and an excellent archaeologist, who appraises artifacts. He does *not* do this to encourage looting, but to save collections for scientific purposes. His reasoning is that people who want to donate their collections to museums, for example, should be able to have a legitimate estimate of value for tax purposes. I appreciate his motives and the contribution to Mississippi archaeology that he is thus making. I do not want to discourage people from donating their collections; after all, artifacts do science or the public no good at all by sitting in a shoebox in someone's closet. And people who want to donate their collections to museums or other public institutions are motivated by noble impulses. But I do want to strongly discourage anyone from going out and collecting artifacts for money. That is a bad business all the way around. And if your motives are noble ones, there are much more useful and altruistic ways to collect artifacts. In chapter 13, I will discuss how to make collecting a constructive, rather than a destructive, activity.

CAN THE GOVERNMENT
TAKE MY STUFF AWAY?

I don't quite know where this question comes from, but I certainly get it a lot. Folks apparently are worried that, if they let anyone official know that they have an artifact collection, the state or the federal government will suddenly swoop down and confiscate it. On more than one occasion, I've had people come up to me after talks and say that they had things they wanted to show me but didn't bring because they were afraid their artifacts would be taken away. Having twice been employed by the federal government (once in the military, once with the U.S. Forest Service) and currently being a state employee (at a university), I find this kind of mistrust rather saddening. Obviously, part of the problem is that people aren't familiar with the laws. But remember that they are *your* laws. And if you own a site, those laws should act to protect it, as discussed in the previous chapter.

Can the government take your stuff away? Short answer: no. Long answer: well, yes, but only in the most rare and unlikely of occasions. I will elaborate on this possibility below.

If you have artifacts on your land, to whom do they belong? To you. Not to the federal government, not to the state, not to an Indian tribe, not to a historical society: to you. This is different from many other countries where objects of antiquity *are* considered the property of the state. Landowners in those countries can be compensated for the value of stuff on their land, but the government asserts public ownership. This is essentially the case in England and Mexico, for example, and many other countries as well. The United States is either behind or ahead of the game, depending on how one judges the relative value of individual property rights and the common good. Being a native of Mississippi, I am quite aware that we tend to put the individual first. That's great, as long as the individual has something approaching common sense. There are times, however—like when someone land-levels a mound that has stood unmolested for a thousand years so that they can grow an additional eighth of an acre of rice, or because they need some dirt to fill in a gully, or because they just want to see what's in it—when I wish that more citizens of Mississippi shared my concern for our unique archaeological remains. Because the stuff is yours, you can do pretty much what you want with it. So why choose to destroy it?

There is one exception to the rights of private landowners. As mentioned in the last chapter, it is very much against the law to knowingly disturb human burials, Native American or otherwise. So if you think you have a burial site on your land, please leave it alone! You wouldn't want anyone plowing up your family cemetery, would you? If you let people collect artifacts on your land, remember that they are supposed to have your written permission. And for goodness' sake, don't let anyone dig on your property, because they inevitably will be destroying something of value, probably without even realizing it. Also, they may encounter a grave, and then both of you may have more trouble than you bargained for.

The only way in which the government can exercise control over the stuff on your land is through eminent domain, the same principle that allows the state to acquire land for a highway corridor, for example.

In late 1998, archaeologists at the Mississippi Department of Archives and History received a tip that an Indian mound near Jackson was being destroyed by the development of a subdivision. An anonymous informant had raised the possibility of this happening some months before, but unfortunately did not provide enough information for the archaeologists to be able to track down the developer. Also, although the site had been recorded some years before, the locational information in the records was wrong. Because of these mishaps, destruction of the mound was well under way by the time archaeologists Keith Baca and Douglas Sims arrived on the scene.

What they beheld was a tragic sight indeed. The prehistoric, flat-topped platform mound had been stripped of trees, and heavy machinery had been used to remove the stumps, causing deep gouges. A wide cut had been made into one side of the mound. Efforts to convince the landowner and developer to change their plans were futile. As noted in this book, there are no laws in the United States that prevent people from destroying archaeological sites on private land unless burials are present, and no human bone was evident at the site. The best that the archaeologists could do was to scramble around with a camera, recording what they could and grabbing artifacts and charcoal samples as the mound disappeared beneath the steel teeth of a backhoe. Radiocarbon dating of the charcoal and analysis of the small sample of pottery obtained suggested that the mound was built around A.D. 1200. It had stood, largely unmolested, for eight centuries: in the space of a few hours, it was gone.

This appalling story is all too common in Mississippi and elsewhere. There really is no need for such a tragedy ever to happen again. If you are a property owner or a developer, please consider your options before you destroy an irreplaceable part of Mississippi's past. Those options include selling your site for a fair price or obtaining a tax break by preserving it while retaining ownership. You will find information in this book to help lead you to these options. Please do what you can to help preserve what's left of Mississippi's unique archaeological remains.

Heavy equipment being used to destroy the eight-hundred-year-old Blaine Mound in Hinds County. Because the site was privately owned and no federal money was involved with the development and because no human burials were known to be present, archaeologists were powerless to save this ancient monument. Photo courtesy of the Mississippi Department of Archives and History.

Theoretically, if you had an archaeological site on your land that was of monumental importance—a major Civil War battlefield, say, or some other truly extraordinary site—then the state or federal government could exert eminent domain and take the property in the name of the public good. In fact, this has gone beyond the theoretical in some rare circumstances: some of our nation's largest Civil War battlefields were acquired through a process of condemnation, for example. In such rare instances, the landowner receives due compensation. But even as an archaeologist who recognizes the importance of Mississippi's cultural remains, I would shy away from the use of this method except in the most extreme cases. There are precious few archaeologists in the state, all working hard to try to educate the public about the importance of our common material legacy. This book is just such an effort. How much good will do you think we would generate if the state were going around grabbing land or artifacts from people?

One of the nicest things about doing archaeology in Mississippi is that people usually are extremely gracious when we ask for permission to work on their lands. Sometimes, it is the landowners themselves who initiate contact, often with surprising results. Some years ago, for example, a landowner in Claiborne County contacted the Mississippi Department of Archives and History. He was curious about some beautiful, polished stone beads and other artifacts he was finding on his land. He suspected that he had something important, and he was right. The state contacted Dr. Phil Carr, of the University of South Alabama, who conducted work at the site with his students. They found evidence of a Middle to Late Archaic–period bead-making industry at the site, an industry that must have combined incredible skill with a technology of breathtaking precision. Small pieces of gravel were knapped into bead blanks with three or four flaked sides. These blanks were then ground and polished into tubular shape and drilled with tiny, gravel chert microdrills. The drills are long, slender things, some no big-

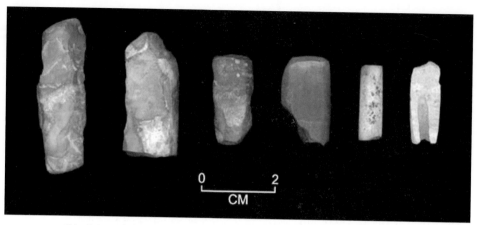

This photograph shows the sequence of manufacture of stone beads from pieces of gravel; the artifacts are from a prehistoric site in Claiborne County, and were brought to the attention of archaeologists by the landowner. Photo courtesy of Phil Carr.

ger around than a grain of rice. How these exquisite tools were hafted and used to drill through the tough gravel beads is still not really understood. We have only just begun to recognize the remains of this surprising behavior from thousands of years ago, and we are still far from explaining it. In this case, the interested landowner put archaeologists on to something of critical importance.

Archaeologists' best hope for preserving sites and learning more about the past is to work with landowners, developers, and other people in whose hands the fate of the archaeological record of Mississippi lies. If you yourself are a landowner, you should take this responsibility seriously. Is it *really* necessary to level that mound to grow another few bushels of rice? Or are you just asserting your right to be able to destroy something on your land if that's what you decide to do? What are your other options?

As it happens, there are other options, and some very good ones at that. If you have an important site on your land, you can request (via the Mississippi Department of Archives and History) that it be designated a *Mississippi Landmark*, a move that will afford it some protection in the future (any activities that might damage the site would require a permit by the state). The site is still yours; it doesn't belong to the state. But its landmark status will be noted on the deed. This is a good way to help prevent the site from being destroyed after you are gone. The department also holds donated preservation easements on several sites, and can be contacted if you'd like to extend that sort of protection to a site on your property (see chapter 14 for contact information).

An even more attractive option, perhaps, is to sell your site. The *Archaeological Conservancy* is an organization that purchases or accepts donations of sites for the purposes of preservation. They are good folks to work with; they are open and honest, and they have already done invaluable service in preserving sites in Mississippi. In fact, one of the first sites that the Conservancy ever purchased in the Southeast was in Oktibbeha County, Mississippi. It was my privilege to be involved with that arrangement, whereby a beautiful, two-thousand-year-old burial mound was bought from a landowner who was selling her property and was concerned about the fate of the site. She contacted archaeologists at Mississippi State University, the archaeologists contacted the Conservancy, representatives came out to look at the property, and they liked what they saw. The landowner sold her land for a fair price, and a very important site was saved for all the citizens of Mississippi to enjoy. Had she sold her land to a private developer or to any other private body, who knows what might have happened to the mound? The Conservancy also has acquired important sites in Coahoma, Jackson, Humphreys, and Tunica counties. In Union County, they acquired the Ingomar Mounds site that I have already mentioned more than once. They are always looking to find more, so if you are interested, you should get in touch with them (contact information is given in chapter 14).

Imagine a conversation being held between your great-grandchildren decades from now. Will they say, "We had an Indian mound on our family land, once, but our great-granddad tore it down"? Or will they say, "Oh yes, we have a mound on our property. Our great-granddad saved it. Come on, let's go see"?

Which is the legacy for which you would like to be remembered?

WHAT HAPPENS
TO THE ARTIFACTS?

Several years ago, I got into a rather heated debate over the difference between archaeologists and pothunters. I was incensed when someone compared the two, as I was an idealistic young student who abhorred the destruction of the archaeological record caused by indiscriminate looting, treasure dives on sunken ships, the defacing of Mayan temples for art that winds up in private collections, and the like. At some point during the conversation, my contender demanded to know if I didn't "want all the artifacts" that were out there. This question caught me completely off guard; I had no idea what to answer. It had never crossed my mind to "want" the stuff. Archaeologists don't collect artifacts to keep. Artifacts are just things, interesting in themselves if you are a collector (as I was when I was a boy), but still just things from which you can't really learn much. If you took all the artifacts from Pompeii and piled them up, what would you have? A really, really big pile of Roman artifacts. Interesting, but pretty much worthless from a scientific viewpoint. It is because the *relationships between the artifacts* are preserved that Pompeii is one of the most spectacular and important archaeological sites in the world. As I worked to become an archaeologist, the thirst for knowledge quickly replaced the desire to "have" the artifacts, and the acquisition of knowledge is, for me, much more fulfilling than simply acquiring stuff. An artifact out of context is like a tooth out of a socket: painful to look at and you can feel that something is missing. I prefer to leave the teeth in place and see if we can get the past to smile back at us.

So, if archaeologists aren't interested in owning the stuff that they pick up or excavate, what happens to it? Well, that's taken care of by the legal system that we have in place. Federal laws not only mandate that archaeology be done when public money is spent on development, but they also insure that the artifacts, as well as photographs, notes, and other records, are saved for all people, for all time. How is this done? By *curation*, the long-term storage of artifacts and documents.

Curation sounds simple, but in actuality it is fairly complicated. How do you store artifacts so that they don't break, rot away, or otherwise become degraded? Put them in bags, for starters, and then into a box. And then into a building. But not just any bags, boxes, or buildings, for there are many considerations that come into play. Not all bags are created equal, for example. Paper bags are slightly acidic, and if you store bone or shell artifacts in them, those artifacts eventually begin to break down. So certain kinds of plastic bags are better, especially ones with labeling blocks where the site number and other information can be recorded in archival-quality ink so that the lettering doesn't fade. Boxes also can be acidic, so special ones are designed that are acid-free. There are other things to think about as well. For example, if you put a bunch of stone tools into a bag, and they get shaken around every time you move them, guess what? Lots of tiny flakes will pop off as the points clack together, thus lessening any chance that the tools' functions could be determined by studying their edges under a microscope. The whole idea behind curation is to keep the collections in as good a shape as possible, and to not lose the provenience information that makes the artifacts important in the first place.

Once the artifacts are bagged and boxed, they are stored (ideally) in a special building where the temperature and humidity are controlled and where there is fire protection. This method of curation is a major advance over how things used to be. Many early archaeological collections, including some truly spectacular ones from Mississippi, have been lost because they were improperly stored or because the buildings they were in burned down. This is a great loss because, in many cases, the collections and records made by archaeologists are all that remain of a site that has since been destroyed. Obviously, we shouldn't let the stuff from the site get destroyed as well. That's why we have regulations that spell out how we are to take care of the collections.

Some stuff takes special care. For example, as most people know, photographs will fade with exposure to light, so photographs of archaeological projects or photographs that are themselves of historical value are kept in special plastic sleeves or other containers in a dark cabinet. Archaeological field forms, though not the most exciting reading material in the world, are very important records of what archaeologists saw as they dug. Copies of such records are made on acid-free paper and are likewise kept out of the light.

Curation is really its own kind of science, and as with all science, we are learning how to do it better all the time. For example, some years ago, Native American religious specialists were examining some wooden artifacts in a national museum to see if they were objects that should be repatriated. The artifacts had been collected decades before, and had been on display since that time. Soon after handling the objects, the specialists fell mysteriously ill. It seems that no one had remembered that, back when they were first put on display, the wood had been treated with an arsenic solution to prevent attack by insects or fungi! In curation, as with everything, archaeologists have to think in the long term.

Wooden artifacts these days are generally treated with a mixture of water and a chemical called polyethylene glycol, or PEG for short. The artifacts are allowed to soak for a long time in the PEG solution, which gradually permeates the cells and prevents decay after the artifacts are dried. PEG can be used on artifacts of all sizes. Remember the celt from the Black Warrior River in Alabama, found still in its wooden handle? It (the handle, that is) was treated with PEG. At the other end of the scale, one of the most glorious things that I have ever seen was in Stockholm, Sweden, where the seventeenth-century warship *Vasa* was found on the bottom of the harbor, still lying where she had sunk on her maiden voyage on August 10, 1628. An innovative design had gone catastrophically wrong for the Swedish Royal Navy, and a huge military investment was lost when the ship went down. In April 1961 the ship was refloated and towed into port, where a special museum to house it was built. The clever conservators rigged up a sprinkler system over the ship and showered it at intervals with a PEG solution for years. Between treatments, the ship was heated with blow dryers to help the solution penetrate the wood. The result? A magnificent, ornately adorned royal vessel with a rich, golden-brown hue that literally glows. I've been privileged to see some amazing archaeological sites in many different parts of the world—Stonehenge in England, Upper Paleolithic cave paintings in Spain, ancient city sites in Israel—but nothing has ever made my jaw drop quite like the *Vasa*. It remains the largest single object ever to be thus preserved.

Fortunately, you don't have to go to Sweden to see a boat preserved with PEG—we have an excellent example right here in Mississippi. Over the decades, a number of whole or fragmentary canoes have been found eroding out of riverbanks in the state, especially in south Mississippi. In 1989, a twenty-five-foot-long dugout canoe, made from a single bald cypress tree, was found when the U.S. Army Corps of Engineers was conducting dredging operations in Steele Bayou, in Washington County. An archaeological team from Louisiana was called in to excavate this incredible find, which was radiocarbon-dated to the mid-eighteenth century. The canoe was in such excellent condition from being buried in muck that the excavators were literally able to float it to a landing, where it was loaded on a flatbed truck and driven to the Yazoo National Wildlife Refuge. There, the canoe was submerged in a pond to prevent deterioration until it could be preserved. Preservation was accomplished by placing the canoe in a metal tank and covering it with a PEG bath for about four years. It then was allowed to dry slowly for another eighteen months, following which it was

Archaeologists recover a wooden canoe from Steele Bayou in Washington County. This ancient watercraft is approximately two hundred and fifty years old, and has been carefully preserved with chemicals. Photo courtesy of the Mississippi Department of Archives and History.

very carefully moved to the Old Capitol Museum in Jackson, where it is currently on display. You just never know what's going to turn up in this business.

But back to curation. Once artifact collections have been curated, who can get access to them? The answer is, anyone with a legitimate use for them, whether that use is research, teaching, or educational displays. In a very real sense, the artifacts belong to all citizens, as taxpayers fund much of the archaeology that is done in this country, one way or another. In practice, there are some hoops to jump through, as curation is both a legal and an ethical responsibility. It's not likely that artifact collections would be loaned out to a Cub Scout group, for example. But it's possible, depending on what artifacts they wanted to borrow, why they wanted to borrow them, and whether an adult was there to sign and be responsible for them. Certainly loans could be made to teachers or to museums, and, of course, to archaeologists who want to do further study of the artifacts. This is particularly important because there is always more that we can learn from any collection of artifacts, and there are many collections that have yet to be studied in detail.

The amount of paperwork involved in a loan depends on where the artifacts are curated and by whom. At Mississippi State University, for example, there is a curation facility erected under contract with the U.S. Army Corps of Engineers. It was built to house the many boxes of artifacts obtained from excavations along the Tennessee-Tombigbee Waterway in Mississippi when that massive construction effort was under way. Many other collections are stored there as well. If one wanted to borrow materials from a Corps project, one would have to meet their particular loan requirements. These might include a written proposal for what would be done with the materials, a timetable for the loan, security arrangements for the collections while on loan, and so on.

One of the most difficult things to get permission to do is destructive analysis, especially if human bones are involved. From a purely scientific viewpoint this is unfortunate, as there is a tremendous amount that can be learned about past lifeways through, for example, the analysis of carbon isotopes in bones, the proportions of which vary depending on the type of diet people had. There are, however, many sound ethical, moral, and political reasons why such scientific concerns must be balanced with other views. These are, after all, the remains of people that we are talking about. As part of a balanced view, it should be kept in mind that there are some very important things that can *only* be investigated via destructive analyses, and that with care, the amount of bone needed can be quite small. The knowledge that results may, in some cases, be applicable to contemporary questions of affiliation, as when remains of undetermined age are radiocarbon-dated, for example. It is to be hoped that, by working together, archaeologists and Native Americans can continue to find constructive ways to move forward on this and other fronts.

An unfortunate truth is that the archaeological record is disappearing. Try as we may to get ahead of the destruction, there are fewer sites in the world every day. The collections that archaeologists obtain, and the records that accompany those collections, represent small but vitally important samples of that vanishing record. Curation is therefore as important as anything that archaeologists do. And it's a sure bet that archaeologists in the future will increasingly turn to the shelves, in addition to the shovels, as they continue to explore the distant frontiers of time.

HOW DO YOU BECOME
AN ARCHAEOLOGIST?

In 1984, I was roofing for a living. "Living" is rather a euphemism, actually; it's been a long while since I read Dante, but I'm pretty sure one of his circles must have included a hot asphalt roof in a Mississippi summer. That particularly nasty job was only the latest in a series of nasty jobs that I had held after obtaining an honorable discharge from the U.S. Air Force. Among my lesser accomplishments as a young adult: installing satellite dishes, being an unsalaried TV repairman, making really, really bad music videos in Nashville, and working the graveyard shift in a suburban convenience store. All of these enterprises paid poorly, and none of them offered me anything resembling a reliable future. So one day I climbed down from a roof, got into my barely functioning, obscenely yellow Datsun B-210, and drove forty miles to the nearest university. I had visited there many years before during a junior high school field trip, and I remembered one building that had caught my eye: an archaeological institute with stone columns out front and arcane symbols from foreign lands carved in bas relief around the door. Nothing in life had interested me nearly as much as arrowheads and the like. I suspected that archaeology was a rarified field—but *some-*

body had to do it, right? So why not me? If I were going to be poor anyway, I reasoned, I might as well be poor doing something that I liked.

By great good fortune, I had arrived just in time to sign up for a summer field school, which meant that my first experience would be working at an actual archaeological site. I never looked back. That first summer I excavated at a prehistoric rock quarry near Meridian, in Lauderdale County, and helped to find nearly one hundred previously unknown sites in Union and Pontotoc counties. As I worked, I began to realize four things that would shape my future: 1) I really, really liked doing archaeology; 2) there were, in fact, many jobs to be had in the field; 3) contrary to what many people believe, everything hasn't already been found, dug up, or figured out; and 4) I was going to spend the rest of my life learning. Learning, it turns out, is like a drug: the more you do it, the more you want. And I was hooked from day one.

When I announced my intention to become an archaeologist, a lot of very well-meaning people whose opinions I respected tried to talk me out of it. Actually, some had been trying to talk me out of it for years. As a senior in high school, for example, I wanted to do something with the prehistoric artifacts from our farm for my science fair project. "Archaeology isn't science," my teacher sniffed disdainfully, and that put paid to that. She was wrong, of course—archaeology certainly tries to be a science—but I didn't really know that at the time. After I started college, my parents tactfully suggested that I keep my hand in at TV repair, "just in case." Good advice, no doubt, but fortunately I was too stubborn to take it. There is room in the world for a great many archaeologists yet, and as I've said, we've barely begun to find and understand what's out there. So if you, too, have the bug, and if you're willing to work hard and take it all seriously, then there is no reason why you shouldn't consider taking up archaeology as a career.

So how do you go about becoming an archaeologist? As with any science, you have to go to college. In this country, that means majoring in anthropology, literally the study of humans. Archaeology is one of the subfields of anthropology, a very broad discipline that also includes cultural anthropology (the study of living cultures), biological anthropology (the study of the biological history of humans), and linguistics (the study of language). Although not everything that one learns in these other subfields is directly relevant to a career in archaeology, there is nothing better than a degree in anthropology to make one think about the world in broader terms. And that is definitely useful when your job is to investigate the unknown.

There are different levels of college degrees that one can get. A Bachelor of Arts, or B.A., is the first, and it takes about four years. If you get a B.A. in anthropology, specializing in archaeology, you can find work, but it is hard to find good, permanent jobs. The work at that level is mostly as a field technician, someone who knows how to do archaeological survey or dig sites properly under supervision. This is great fun, but the work tends to be seasonal because, like roofing, field archaeology tends to slow down in the winter.

A typical course of study at the B.A. level includes some of the basics of a liberal arts education: low-level math, a foreign language, English composition, public speaking, and so on. Electives can be chosen that pertain to archaeology, such as geology, cultural geography, soil science, and history. Taking some computer classes certainly doesn't hurt. And if you're really determined to get ahead of the pack, you might take classes in land surveying, chemistry, photography, statistics, and other areas to pick up some useful skills. The anthropology courses are designed to give you some knowledge of all the subfields, so you might take Introduction to Anthropology, Introduction to Cultural Anthropology, Introduction to Archaeology, Introduction to Biological Anthropology, and perhaps a linguistics course. You also will get some higher-level courses, like North American Archaeology, Rise of Civilization, or North American Indians. The main skills that one needs to acquire at the bachelor's level are thinking critically (when you read a book or an article, what is the author *really* trying to say?) and writing clearly (when you write a class paper, what are you *really* trying to say?). It's very much a growing process, and students who are willing to work hard can definitely pick up a lot in a good B.A. program.

The second level of college degrees is a master's degree, usually a Master of Arts, or M.A. This is where the jobs are. As I discussed earlier, a lot of archaeology takes place because the law says that it will. There are companies that specialize in taking care of this kind of work, in which construction zones must be surveyed for sites, and significant sites must be dug, before construction can take place. This process is called *cultural resources management,* or CRM, and CRM archaeologists are hired on a contract basis just as construction companies are. Most states have regulations stating that people who oversee contract archaeology must have the proper qualifications, a reasonable enough precaution given what is at stake. So what makes one qualified? You guessed it—a master's degree in anthropology or some closely related field. These M.A.-level jobs are very demanding: to do them well, one must be a combination scientist, businessman, engineer, mechanic, politician, accountant, and psychologist (you have to keep your crew happy!). But they also pay pretty well and provide decent job security. Most of the good archaeology jobs that are out there are in CRM, and we desperately need good people to fill them. It takes another two to three years after the B.A. to get an M.A., so seven years is the typical investment to become a working professional archaeologist.

What kind of courses do you take in a master's program? To some extent, that depends on where you go to get your degree. Typically there will be a course in Archaeological Method and Theory (how things are done, and why), some survey courses at the regional level or higher (North American Archaeology, for example), and some specialized courses related to your chosen subdiscipline (such as Public

Mississippi State University students learning how to excavate at a prehistoric site in Oktibbeha County under the direction of Dr. Janet Rafferty. Photo courtesy of Janet Rafferty.

Mississippi State University student Tom James waterscreening at the Lyon's Bluff site in Oktibbeha County. Archaeology students learn the importance of carefully retrieving artifacts from the soil and keeping track of where those artifacts come from.

Archaeology, Human Osteology, Environmental Archaeology, and Archival Research). And if you haven't taken one yet, you will probably be required to take an archaeological field school, where you are taught the basics of excavation (taught at pretty much every school) and, if you're lucky, site survey (unfortunately, taught at very few schools, for reasons I don't understand). Master's students also begin to develop their own particular research interests while in school, a process culminating in the production of a thesis on some archaeological problem that they try to solve. That's where it gets tough. It's not easy to establish a research question, carry out the field and lab work, analyze the artifacts, and write up the results in a way that will satisfy your committee (a group of professors whose job it is to see you do things well). That's also where it becomes truly rewarding, however, as a good thesis is an original contribution to the field. It is your entryway into the ranks of those of us lucky enough to be archaeological researchers. It is a rite of passage. And it is definitely something of which to be proud.

The next level is the Ph.D., or doctoral degree. This usually takes another several years to complete, probably about five or six on average. A Ph.D. is generally required if you want to teach at a university, and although such academic jobs exist, there aren't very many of them and the competition is accordingly fierce. You have to be pretty determined to succeed at the Ph.D. level, but the rewards (teaching!) can be great. And with a Ph.D. in hand you can still work in CRM. In fact, more and more Ph.D.'s are choosing to enter the commercial arena, where the pay is good and a lot more hands-on archaeology is involved.

In a Ph.D. program, besides taking another suite of courses, you are required to produce a dissertation, which is like a thesis times ten. In essence, writing a dissertation means writing a book; indeed, many dissertations subsequently are published as books. And the special skills that you develop while doing a dissertation may well guide the rest of your career.

If you are interested in becoming an archaeologist, get on the Internet and check out the anthropology program at the state universities. Or make an appointment with an undergraduate advisor, and go check things out for yourself. If you make up your mind to join the field, there is no reason why you yourself can't become a professional archaeologist. And besides being a heck of a lot of fun, it's a pretty cool thing to get to write on your tax forms every year.

WHAT CAN I DO TO HELP?

I'm always gratified when people ask this question. One of the nice things about living and working in the South is that people care about things, especially when they realize that those things are precious and irreplaceable, as are archaeological sites. So in this chapter, I will summarize some of the most important points made thus far, in the form of suggestions. If you follow these suggestions, you can rest assured that you are doing your part to help preserve Mississippi's fascinating archaeological legacy.

If you are an artifact collector, there are some very simple steps that you can take to convert a destructive activity into a constructive one. First of all, keep the artifacts from your different collecting spots separate; don't mix things from different spots together. If you do mix your artifacts, you have just rendered them pretty much worthless from a scientific standpoint. More than once I've talked to collectors who, in their later years, wanted to donate their artifacts to a museum or a university. That impulse is an admirable one, so they are often surprised and hurt when the interest shown in their collection is lukewarm, at best. The problem is that they have mixed everything up, so that the collection is not a source of reliable information, it's just a big pile of stuff. Had they kept the artifacts from their different collection spots separate, then those artifacts could have been used to teach us all kinds of things about the past. What a loss, to throw all that information away because people don't know to keep the artifacts from each spot together! It's a very simple thing to do, but one of profound importance.

Next, get a map! And plot your collection spots on it. Don't rely on memory. Every collector I've ever met has assured me that he knows just where all of his artifacts came from. Unfortunately, that's not good enough. Memory is fallible; I know, because I speak from experience. As a teenager, I collected points from several different sites in northern Mississippi, and there was a time when I indeed knew where each point had been found. But I waited too long, and when I finally sat down to record the sites, I discovered to my chagrin that I could not say for sure which point came from where. I could definitely assign only a few of them (like that first arrowhead I found).

This is a very common problem, as it turns out. Many times I have sat down with collectors and looked at their artifacts—usually dumped out of a bucket or shoebox, sometimes carefully mounted in a nice frame. When pressed, most have confessed that they're *pretty* sure they know where all the things came from. But pretty sure just doesn't cut it. Unless we are *one hundred percent, absolutely* sure that a particular artifact came from a particular site, we can't take the chance of treating it as a piece of scientific data. To do so would be to risk confusion that might never subsequently be straightened out. And, of course, if you don't properly record your collection, no one else will be able to do so when you're gone. So if you are a collector, don't wait until it's too late to let your good impulses take hold! Start right now, with a map and separate containers for your different sites. Give them names of some sort—"A, B, C" will do nicely—and label them accordingly on your maps. An excellent kind of map to use for this purpose is found in the county soil books, available from the Natural Resources Conservation Service office in your county seat. Many of you have collections of hundreds or even thousands of artifacts. Please don't let what those artifacts can tell us be lost.

It helps to take care of your artifacts as well—to curate them, in a sense, in the best fashion that you can. I know one gentleman who showed me a large collection of celts that he had picked up over the years. His innovative way of caring for them? He used them to pave his flower garden. My father once glued several projectile points to a board to display on our mantle. Unfortunately, he used some sort of funky, brown, industrial-strength adhesive that I was never able to scrape completely off afterwards. The worst excuse for taking care of artifacts I ever saw was in a catfish restaurant in north Mississippi, where the enterprising owner had incorporated whole points, celts, grinding stones, and other artifacts into the mortared façade of his fireplace. Presumably, people collect artifacts because they are interested in them. So why take such poor care of something that is important to you? With proper, simple records, as described above, your collections can make a valuable contribution to science. You should treat them accordingly.

The problems caused by buying and selling artifacts have been discussed already, so I won't elaborate too much here. You should be aware, however, that if you insist on buying artifacts, you might well get burned. There are an awful lot of fakes out there on the market, some of which are obvious to a trained eye, but many of which are indistinguishable from the real thing. Also, I will remind you that if you buy a pot or some other really nice artifact, the odds are very high that it came out of a grave, making you accessory to a crime if you purchase it. Finally, remember that, by law, collectors are supposed to have written permission from the landowner to pick stuff up off their land. If someone has artifacts for sale, on the Internet or otherwise, don't take their word that the stuff was acquired legally. Demand to see the signed letter of permission. If they won't produce it, be careful! You might well be dealing with a criminal. And remember that permissions, too, can be faked. The best way to buy artifacts . . . is to not buy artifacts. It's always a questionable business, it's always destructive, and it can get downright sordid. Really, it's better to just stay away from that sort of thing altogether.

If you are a landowner yourself, you probably have sites on your land, in which case you have an opportunity to distinguish yourself as a forward-thinking and responsible citizen. If you know of sites on your land, leave them alone as much as possible: they are "information banks" that may become extremely important in the future. If you are a farmer, please consider carefully how your agricultural practices might affect archaeological resources on your property. If you want to do land leveling or terracing, for example, can you find ways to go around sites and still achieve most of your management aims? If a site has been plowed for years, continued plowing won't really hurt it any further, unless you change the type of plowing so that the disturbance goes deeper. Subsoiling, for example, has an absolutely catastrophic effect on sites.

What if you don't know what's out there on your land? Archaeologists could tell you, but remember that there are darn few of us, and unfortunately we don't have the time to come out and see everybody's stuff, as much as we'd like to. So be patient with us! I have never known an archaeologist who wasn't happy to look at people's artifacts, if they can bring them in. We can then at least tell you what you have and give advice on what to do about it. And who knows? You might have something really spectacular that would cause us to drop everything else and come to see your site. It's happened before! And if you have a nice site on your property, remember your options for preserving it for all time, such as donating it or selling it to the Archaeological Conservancy, having it declared a Mississippi Landmark, or working with the Mississippi Department of Archives and History to get a historic preservation easement.

Finally, one more time: don't dig! If you do, you inevitably will destroy valuable sources of information, such as features, without even knowing it. And you never know when you might hit a burial. If you'd really like to dig up some artifacts, check out the information in the next chapter on the opportunities to do so with a professional archaeologist. Whenever you are dealing with archaeological remains, be they artifacts or sites, remember that you are dealing with something unique, something important, something nonrenewable. You have part of Mississippi in your hands: take care of it!

HOW CAN I LEARN MORE?

There are a number of sources for further information for those interested in the archaeology of Mississippi. The Mississippi Department of Archives and History (MDAH), located in Jackson, is the state agency that deals with matters related to archaeology and historic preservation. The Historic Preservation Division is responsible for insuring compliance with the various federal and state laws related to cultural resources. Members of the division also maintain the inventory of known archaeological sites in the state and nominate significant sites to the National Register of Historic Places. In addition, the department oversees some very important sites that are open to the public, such as the Winterville Mounds and the Grand Village of the Natchez. If you know of a site that is being looted or otherwise destroyed, you can contact MDAH to let them know about it. The phone number is 601-576-6940. Explain the situation, and you will be directed to the proper personnel. MDAH also administers grant programs for communities interested in preserving their historical character, and can provide information on tax breaks for individuals who take steps to preserve archaeological sites or other cultural resources on their lands. The department also has brochures and literature produced for the general public, such as Jim Barnett's excellent overview of the Natchez Indians and Keith Baca's outstanding brochure on Indian mounds in the state. A variety of archaeological topics is covered on their Web site: www.mdah.state.ms.us/hpres/archaeology.html.

The *Mississippi Association of Professional Archaeologists* is just what it sounds like—a professional association for practicing archaeologists in the state. MAPA cooperates with MDAH to organize events for Mississippi Archaeology Month. Currently being held every October, this includes a series of events all over the state that are organized specifically for the public. Events include archaeological digs, public lectures, artifact displays, flintknapping demonstrations, and other proceedings. If you want to become personally involved with the archaeology of Mississippi, then Mississippi Archaeology Month is something you definitely should check out. Pertinent information can be found on the MDAH Web site: www.mdah.state.ms.us.

Also helping with Mississippi Archaeology Month is the *Mississippi Archaeological Association*. The MAA is composed of professional and amateur archaeologists, collectors, and members of the general public who are interested in the archaeology and history of the state. If you're one of those people who, like me, was "runt" after finding that first arrowhead, then you would feel right at home in the MAA. With the assistance of MDAH, the association puts out two issues of an excellent journal, *Mississippi Archaeology*, each year. If you are a teacher, this belongs in your school library! The association also puts out regular newsletters that alert members to digs, talks, museum displays, and other news related to archaeology. Local chapters exist in various parts of the state. Membership dues are quite reasonable, and by joining you not only will gain access to valuable information, but you also will be doing a lot to support archaeology in Mississippi. You can learn more about the MAA from the Web site: www.mdah.state.ms.us/misc/maaflyer.html. To join, print off a membership form and send it with payment to:

Volunteer Chris Brantley learns how to excavate a feature at a PIT project held in the Tombigbee National Forest, Winston County.

Secretary-Treasurer, Mississippi Archaeology Association, P.O. Box 571, Jackson, Mississippi, 39205.

There are archaeologists at Mississippi State University, the University of Mississippi, the University of Southern Mississippi, and Millsaps College. Most are happy to look at artifacts you may want to have identified, to talk to you about majoring in anthropology, or to otherwise share their knowledge. Always best to call first, though, to make sure someone is available! Dial the number for general information at the university, and ask for anthropology. You should be able to find an archaeologist from there. At Mississippi State, you can contact the Cobb Institute of Archaeology (662-325-3826). Richard Marshall's *Indians of Mississippi* is a good, nontechnical guide to the culture history and characteristic artifacts of the state, with many drawings, and can be purchased from the Cobb Institute. The Web site is www.cobb.msstate.edu.

The U.S. Forest Service runs an excellent Heritage Resources program in Mississippi, which includes something called the Passport in Time (PIT) program. This is a program in which you can work on an archaeological excavation or other field project under the supervision of a Forest Service archaeologist. If you want to know what's going on in terms of archaeology in a national forest near you, or if you want to report signs of looting or other damage to archaeological sites to the Forest Service, contact Sam Brookes, Heritage Program Manager, National Forests in Mississippi, 100 West Capitol St., Suite 1141, Jackson, Mississippi, 39202 (phone 601-965-4391).

The Natural Resources Conservation Service (formerly the Soil Conservation Service) is a federal agency dedicated to helping farmers and other landowners conserve the soil, water, and other resources. NRCS projects often fall under the requirements of the National Historic Preservation Act. Farmers who are uncertain about projects on their land, or who wish to know more, can call the Jackson office of the NRCS (601-965-5196) and ask to speak with the archaeologist or the cultural resources office.

The Mississippi Band of Choctaw Indians has a tribal archaeologist who can provide information relating to the Choctaw. Contact Ken Carleton, Mississippi Band of Choctaw Indians, Box 6257, Philadelphia, Mississippi, 39350, or e-mail him at kcarleton@choctaw.org.

The Archaeological Conservancy was founded in the early 1980s as a nationwide, nonprofit organization dedicated to identifying and preserving important archaeological remains by acquiring outright ownership of sites. The organization is funded by membership dues and by contributions from individuals, foundations, and corporations. In addition to purchasing or accepting sites as donations, the Conservancy conducts archaeological tours and publishes an excellent quarterly magazine, *American Archaeology*. There are five regional offices, including one in the Southeast. If you have a site on your land that you consider to be worthy of protection, the Archaeological Conservancy might be interested in accepting it as a donation (tax deductible) or buying it outright. And if you are one of those admirable people who tries to make the world a better place by donating to worthy causes, please consider making a tax-deductible donation to the Conservancy. They've done a lot to help protect the archaeological resources of Mississippi. For the Southeast in general, contact Alan Gruber, Southeast Regional Director, 5997 Cedar Crest Road, Acworth, Georgia, 30101 (phone 770-975-4344; e-mail tacser@aol.com). For Mississippi, contact Jessica Crawford, 225 Crawford Road, Lambert, Mississippi (phone 662-326-6465; e-mail jessicac@gmi.net).

Finally, please feel free to e-mail me if you think I might be able to help you out with a question: peacock@anthro.msstate.edu. Thank you for any effort you can make to help preserve the archaeological record that is our common link to a common humanity.

GLOSSARY

Absolute dating The term referring to a number of different methods for obtaining actual ages in years for artifacts, plant and animal remains, soils, and other materials. Gives a date range within which the phenomenon of interest occurred. See **archaeomagnetism**, **radiocarbon dating**, and **thermoluminescence** dating.

Archaeological Conservancy A nonprofit organization that buys or accepts donations of archaeological sites for the purpose of preserving them.

Archaeological Resources Protection Act (ARPA) A law passed in 1976 that sets fines and penalties for the looting of archaeological sites.

Archaeology The study of artifacts and the relationships between them.

Archaeomagnetism An absolute dating method based on fluctuations in the earth's magnetic field over time.

Archaic period In general, the period of time from about nine thousand to three thousand years ago.

Artifact Anything made or modified by a human being.

Avocational archaeology Also called amateur archaeology. The formal practice of archaeology by nonprofessionals, including the keeping of records about sites, participation in professionally sponsored excavations, and other contributions to the discipline.

Basketloading The method by which prehistoric earthen mounds were built. One basketload of dirt was dumped at a time, then stamped or pounded to pack it down.

Bioturbation Literally, "life mixing." The natural disturbance of soils by the actions of plants and animals.

Bipolar flaking A specialized technique for removing flakes from rocks, involving the use of a hammerstone and stone anvil.

Brick index A measure of how brick sizes change through time, used as a means of dating old building foundations and other brick features at Historic-period sites.

Burial urns Large ceramic vessels in which deceased infants or human bones were placed for burial.

Caches Groups of artifacts purposefully buried together.

Celt A stone axe made by grinding and polishing rather than by flaking.

Conical mounds Prehistoric mounds with rounded tops, often containing human burials. Mostly associated with the Middle Woodland period, some of uncertain function were built much earlier in the Middle Archaic period.

Controlled surface collection (CSC) The process of establishing a grid across a site and collecting artifacts separately from within each grid unit.

Cross-dating A relative dating method, whereby artifacts and sites can be placed in chronological order by reference to the relative depths of distinct styles of artifacts at numerous sites.

Cultural resources management (CRM) The practice of commercial archaeology.

Curation The long-term storage of artifacts and their associated records.

Diagnostic An artifact style considered to be representative of a particular cultural period.

Early Archaic period In general, the period of time from about nine thousand to seven thousand years ago.

Early Woodland period In general, the period of time from about three thousand to two thousand years ago. Mostly used in the northern part of the state. "Gulf Formational period" used elsewhere.

Ethnoarchaeology The study of artifacts and features left by contemporary groups of people.

Experimental archaeology The practice of creating artifacts and features through the use of traditional methods in order to better understand how they were made, used, and discarded.

Features Nonportable artifacts, such as fire hearths, garbage pits, burials, postholes, and foundations.

Fire hearth A place where a controlled fire burned in the past, recognized by the presence of ash, charcoal, and changes in the soil color caused by heat.

Flakes Pieces struck off a rock during flintknapping. Sometimes called "chips" by nonarchaeologists.

Flintknapping The process of making flaked-stone tools with traditional methods.

General surface collection (GSC) Collecting artifacts from a site without keeping track of where they came from on that site.

Greenstone A green-colored, metamorphic rock that was shaped into celts and other smooth-surfaced artifacts. See **celt**.

Grinding stone A slab of coarse-grained rock, usually sandstone, used to grind up seeds and other plant foods. Sometimes called a "metate."

Ground-penetrating radar (GPR) A geophysical device used to image objects and features underneath the ground by emitting waves and reading the reflections.

Gulf Formational period See Early Woodland period.

Hammerstone A hard, dense rock, usually quartzite, used to strike other rocks during flintknapping. Recognized by the characteristic, battered wear pattern.

Historic period In general, the period of time in Mississippi from about three hundred years ago until today.

Hypsithermal A warmer, drier climatic episode lasting approximately from eight thousand to five thousand years ago.

Late Archaic period In general, the period of time from about five thousand to three thousand years ago.

Late Woodland period In general, the period of time from about fourteen hundred to one thousand years ago.

Law of Superposition A principle which states that, in a set of depositional strata, artifacts or layers lower in the ground are older than artifacts or layers less deep in the ground.

Magnetometry A geophysical method for imaging objects and features under the ground by registering changes in the residual magnetic signature of the soil.

Mastodons An extinct form of elephant that lived in Mississippi during the last Ice Age.

Midden A kind of soil characteristic of long-term habitation sites that is dark in color and contains an abundance of artifacts.

Middle Archaic period In general, the period of time from about seven thousand to five thousand years ago.

Middle Woodland period In general, the period of time from about two thousand to fourteen hundred years ago.

Mississippi Archaeological Association An organization dedicated to the preservation and better understanding of Mississippi's archaeological resources. Made up of a mix of professional and avocational archaeologists, artifact collectors, and interested members of the public.

Mississippi Association of Professional Archaeologists A professional organization made up of practicing archaeologists in Mississippi.

Mississippi Department of Archives and History The state agency charged with oversight of cultural resources management in Mississippi.

Mississippi period In general, the period of time from about one thousand to five hundred years ago. Also called the Mississippian period.

Mitigation Lessening the impact of construction or other destructive forces on archaeological sites by taking steps to protect the sites or by excavating sites prior to destruction to save the information they contain.

National Register of Historic Places A list administered by the National Park Service of places considered to be of historic or cultural significance.

Native American Graves Protection and Repatriation Act (NAGPRA) A law passed in 1990 that required agencies or institutions receiving federal funding to report all human burials and associated items to any Native American groups who requested the information.

Nonrenewable resource A resource that cannot be increased through management, such as archaeological sites.

Occupation The artifacts deposited by a group of people over a continuous period of site use.

Open-field survey A systematic walk through plowed agricultural fields or other exposed ground for the finding and recording of archaeological sites. Also called "pedestrian survey."

Paleo-Indian period In general, the period of time from about fourteen thousand to nine thousand years ago.

Palisade A defensive, wooden wall built around a site to protect the inhabitants from attack.

Percussion flaking The process of removing flakes from a rock by striking it with another object. See **hammerstone** and **flintknapping**.

Pitted stone A coarse-grained stone, usually sandstone, with one or more small depressions in one or both sides.

Platform mounds Rectangular, flat-topped mounds characteristic of the Mississippi period, during which time they supported wooden temples or other structures. Flat-topped mounds also were built during the Middle and Late Woodland periods, but their function is currently uncertain.

Post holes Cylindrical stains in the soil that mark where a wooden post was once set.

Pothunters People who loot archaeological sites for profit.

Preform An object produced during the manufacture of stone tools by flint-knapping. It represents an early stage in the production of a spear point, for example. Preforms typically are flaked on both surfaces. Whole and broken preforms of various stages of manufacture are commonly found at archaeological sites in the Southeast.

Pressure flaking The process of removing very small flakes from the edge of a stone tool by pressing against the tool edge with a deer antler tine or other object. See **flintknapping**.

Profile A wall, or the drawing of a wall, of an excavation unit. Also refers to the drawing of a feature from the side once one half of the feature has been excavated.

Projectile point A spear or arrow point. Usually made of stone, but sometimes made of bone or other materials.

Protohistoric period In general, the time period from about five hundred to three hundred years ago.

Provenience An artifact's location in three dimensions when it is recorded.

Radiocarbon dating An absolute dating method based upon the radioactive decay of carbon 14, an unstable isotope.

Random sampling Blindly choosing targets, a certain number of which are supposed to represent all the targets in the universe of interest. If an archaeologist could only dig five percent of a large site, for example, he or she might randomly choose where to dig to try to get a good idea of everything that's at the site. See **representative sample**.

Relative dating Arranging events represented by artifacts, strata, or sites through time relative to one another; does not give an actual age, but allows archaeologists to see which thing is older or younger than other things.

Repatriation Returning human burials and associated artifacts to Native American tribes or other groups who can demonstrate a historical link with those materials.

Representative sample A collection of artifacts that is assumed to give a good picture of the different kinds and proportions of all artifacts from a particular site.

Sedentariness "Settling down." At least part of the population lives at a site throughout the year.

Seriation A relative dating method by which artifact assemblages are ordered through time based on changing styles.

Settlement patterns How sites approximately the same age, and presumably of the same cultural tradition, are distributed upon the landscape.

Shell mounds Archaeological sites with thick strata containing lots of freshwater mussel or other shellfish remains.

Sherds Broken pieces of ceramic pottery, as in glass "shards."

Shovel-test survey The process of finding sites in wooded or other vegetated areas by digging small holes in the ground and screening the dirt for artifacts.

Side-scan sonar A remote sensing method used to find shipwrecks by detecting sound echoes.

Significance A property ascribed by archaeologists to sites that denotes those sites' importance.

Site Any place where artifacts are found.

Site function A term referring to the activities that were carried out at a site.

Site survey The process of finding and recording archaeological sites.

Smudge pit A small pit dug into the ground into which corncobs were packed and burned to produce smoke.

Soapstone A soft, gray, metamorphic rock that can be easily carved into bowls, pipes, or other artifacts.

Soil conductivity A property of the soil; how well it conducts an electrical current.

Soil resistivity A property of the soil; how well it resists conducting an electrical current.

Soto, Hernando de A Spanish conquistador who, with his army, was the first European to travel through interior Mississippi, in the years A.D. 1540–1541.

Special-purpose sites Sites where only, or primarily, specific tasks were carried out (a hunting camp, for example).

Sterile Lacking artifacts.

Stratum A layer in the soil.

Temper Material added to pottery clay to improve the qualities of the vessel.

Test excavation An archaeological excavation that is purposefully limited in scope. Usually designed to provide some basic information about a site in order to determine that site's significance. See **significance**, and compare to **mitigation**.

Thermoluminescence dating An absolute dating method based on the principle that decaying radioactive isotopes in clays store energy over time. When heated to a sufficient temperature, sherds release the stored energy, which can be measured to provide a date range within which the pot was originally fired. Also works on stone or other materials that have been heated to a sufficient temperature in the past.

Transects Lines along which sites are sampled or surveys are conducted.

Triangular point Small projectile points used to tip arrows. Commonly called "bird points" by nonarchaeologists, but used for all game.

Wall trenches Narrow ditches dug to support wooden posts for house walls or defensive barriers. See **palisade**.

INDEX

chips. *See* flakes
Choctaw: tribe, 49, 66; Mississippi Band of, 134
Choctaw County, 3, 7, 12, 85
Chakchiuma tribe, 66
cisterns, 10, 19, 68
Civil War battlefields, 23, 24, 101, 108. *See also* Vicksburg National Military Park
Claiborne County, 108–9
Clarksdale bell, 64
Coahoma County, 56, 64, 110
Cobb Institute of Archaeology, 133
collecting, artifact, 43–44, 85, 87, 91, 96–98, 101, 104, 106, 112, 126–28, 132
collectors. *See* collecting
conductivity. *See* remote sensing
Connaway, John, 97
consultation, between archaeologists and Native Americans, 45–46, 103
copper, 43, 70
corn. *See* maize
Corps of Engineers, U.S. Army, 116–17
Crawford, Jessica, 135
Culpepper, Lacey, 27
cultural resources management (CRM), 122, 124
curation, 101, 113–18, 128

Dalton culture, 51
dating. *See* absolute dating; archaeo-magnetism; radiocarbon dating; relative dating; seriation; thermolu-minescence dating
Denton site, 5
digs. *See* excavation
dinosaurs, 93
dogtrot cabin, 23
drills, stone, 22, 108
Dunnell, Robert, 16

Elliott, Jack, 41
Emerald Mounds site, 64
end scrapers, 51
England, English, 71, 80, 106, 115
ethnoarchaeology, 11
excavation, 11, 22, 24, 25, 28, 30, 45–47, 49, 58, 73, 76, 79, 80–82, 87, 116, 120–22, 124, 132, 134
experimental archaeology, 11

fish weirs, 53
flakes, 11, 20, 22, 26, 39, 53, 76, 88, 91–92, 113
flintknapping, 11, 86, 88–89, 108, 132
Ford, James A., 36
Forest Service, U.S., 8, 10, 21, 47, 73–74, 80, 105, 134
fossils, 93
France, French, 66, 71–72

Galloway, Patricia, 61
Geiger, Carey, 97
Giliberti, Joseph, 97
Goodyear, Al, 97
graves, 19, 26, 44–46, 61–62, 65, 69, 70, 72, 74, 83, 87, 95–96, 99–100, 102–4, 106–7, 110, 117–18, 130. *See also* cemeteries
Great Depression, 48, 68
Great Sun, 71. *See also* Natchez
grinding stones, 22, 92, 93, 128
Gruber, Alan, 135
Gulf Coast Research Laboratory, 97
Gulf Formational period. *See* Woodland period, Early

hammerstone, 88–89, 92
Hancock County, 83
hearth features, 16, 27–28, 38, 40, 76
Hinds County, 107

Historic period, 49, 51, 66–68
Humphreys County, 110
hunter-gatherers, 11, 32, 57, 61
Hypsithermal, 52

Ice Age, 15, 50–51
Indians, prehistoric: agriculture, 53, 58,
    62, 77, 89; architecture, 57, 59, 62–63,
    70–72, 76, 89; hunting and fishing,
    51–53, 56–58, 61–62, 87, 91, 93; impact
    of diseases on, 65; religious special-
    ists, 114–15; settlement patterns, 17,
    57–62, 65; trade, 43, 55, 60, 89, 90;
    villages, 16, 22, 24, 28, 59, 83, 98; war-
    fare, 28, 61–63, 71, 87, 90
Indians of Mississippi, 133
Ingomar Mounds site, 5, 17, 72–73, 79,
    110
Iroquois, 89

Jackson, Ed, 82, 97
Jackson County, 27, 110
Jackson's Landing site, 83
Jaketown site, 5
James, Tom, 123
Jenkins, Cliff, 67
jobs in archaeology, 18, 22, 119–25
Johnson, Jay, 28, 73
Josephine, 5, 29

Kosciusko quartzite, 4, 6

landowners, 17, 19, 22, 28, 44, 73,
    95–96, 98, 102, 104–10, 128–29
Lauderdale County, 120
laws, historic preservation, 8–9, 18, 23,
    44–45, 94–96, 100, 102–7, 113, 122,
    128, 131, 134
Lee County, 19, 54
Lincoln County, 84

Little Spanish Fort site, 5, 81–83
looting, 46, 100–3, 112, 134. *See also*
    laws, historic preservation;
    pothunting
Lowndes County, 54, 59
Lyon's Bluff site, 5, 27–28, 34, 63, 79,
    98, 123

magnetometry. *See* remote sensing
Mainfort, Robert, 72
maize, 13, 53, 62, 77, 89. *See also*
    Indians, prehistoric, agriculture
Marshall, Richard, 133
Marshall County, 18, 33, 47
mastodons, 51–52
McGahey, Sam, 32, 97
metal detecting, 101–2
metate. *See* grinding stones
Michie, James, 97
midden, 52, 54, 96, 98
Millsaps College, 133
Minerals Management Service, U.S., 29
Mississippi Archaeological
    Association, 97, 132–33
Mississippi Archaeology, 97, 132
Mississippi Archaeology Month, 97,
    132
Mississippi Association of Professional
    Archaeologists, 132
Mississippi Department of Archives
    and History (MDAH), 4, 61, 81, 92,
    97, 102, 107–9, 129, 131–32
Mississippi Department of
    Transportation, 16, 84
Mississippi Landmark, 110, 129
Mississippi period, 34, 36, 50–51,
    62–65, 72–73, 79, 98
Mississippi Projectile Point Guide, 32
Mississippi State University, 17, 19–20,
    27–28, 41, 73, 76, 110, 117, 123, 133

shell mounds, 57–58
sherds. *See* pottery
shipwrecks, 27, 29–30, 103, 112, 115
significance, 22–24
Sims, Douglas, 107
Slate Springs Mound site, 72
slaves, slavery, 66–67
soapstone, 56
Soto, Hernando de, 64–65, 72. *See also* Spaniards, Spanish
Spaniards, Spanish, 64–65, 72, 82. *See also* Soto, Hernando de
spear points, 11, 16, 22, 31, 38, 51–54, 56, 83, 85–86, 88–89, 91, 96, 99. *See also* projectile points
surface collection, 11, 19, 25–26, 99, 102. *See also* survey
survey: archaeological, 15, 18, 22, 103, 121, 122, 124; open field, 15, 17, 20; shovel test, 15, 21, 47, 76. *See also* surface collection

Tatooed Serpent, 71. *See also* Natchez
tax breaks, 104, 107, 131, 135
thermoluminescence dating, 39. *See also* absolute dating
tomahawks, 89–90. *See also* celt
triangular points. *See* arrow points
tribes, 103, 105. *See also individual Indian tribes*
Tuma, Michael, 67
Tunica County, 63, 110
Tunica tribe, 66

Union County, 17, 20, 54, 60, 72–73, 79, 110, 120
United Nations Educational, Scientific, and Cultural Organization (UNESCO), 103
University of Mississippi, 28, 73, 133
University of South Alabama, 108

University of South Carolina, 97
University of Southern Mississippi, 66–67, 82, 97, 133
U.S.S. *Cairo*, 102

Vicksburg National Military Park, 5, 102

Warren County, 36
Washington County, 116
Watson Brake site, 83
Webb, Clarence, 97
Winschel, Terry, 102
Winston County, 21, 72, 133
Winterville Mounds site, 5, 62, 131
Woodland period, 50; Early, 50–51, 57, 59–60; Middle, 50–51, 60–62, 69–70, 72–73, 79, 81–83; Late, 6, 50–51, 61–62, 86–87

Yazoo tribe, 66
Young, Amy, 66–67